SAFE
AT
HOME

By
Betsy Myers

Armstrong Publishing Co.

We sincerely appreciate the help and cooperation of the following agencies:

Chicago Fire Department
Chicago Police Department
Dallas Crime Prevention Unit
Dallas Fire Prevention Unit
Dallas Office of Emergency Preparedness
Los Angeles Chapter American Red Cross
Los Angeles Police Department (Crime Prevention Unit)
Miami Crime Prevention Unit
Sacramento City Fire Department
San Diego Fire Department
San Diego Police Department
San Francisco Fire Department
State of California Office of Emergency Services
St. Louis Crime Prevention Unit

SAFE AT HOME
By Betsy Myers

TABLE OF CONTENTS

SAFETY FIRST, LAST AND ALWAYS...

The prevention tactics in this book will go a long way towards reducing your risk of becoming a victim and then just a statistic. For what doesn't show up in crime, accident and disaster reports is the awful knowledge that your house, person or valuable property has been invaded, the time and effort of filing an insurance report, the trouble of repairing the damage, and the irreplaceable loss of life and property.

This book will show you:
- practical and inexpensive ways to safeguard yourself, your family, your personal property and your home,
- how to prepare for and act in the event of natural disasters,
- how to keep yourself alert,
- how to lessen the risk of personal harm and minimize property damage.

By taking personal responsibility for our safety, we also help our police, fire and disaster agencies in their fight to protect our homes and lives. As the experts will testify, it's up to each of us — civil authorities and citizen alike — to join efforts in the battle for safe, secure homes and streets. We must be the ones to provide at least basic protection for our homes and our lives. If there's no place like home, then let's make sure it's a safe, secure place to dwell.

CHAPTER 1

THE CRIME STATISTICS IN THE UNITED STATES — WILL YOU BECOME ONE?

What are the chances you or someone you know will be the target of a burglary, robbery or theft this year? According to the most recent U.S. Department of Justice's FBI Uniform Crime Report, 4,629.5 crimes against property (burglary, theft and motor vehicle theft) per 100,000 population were committed in 1983. That means slightly less than five persons in 100 or one in 20 becomes the victim of such crimes. If other major offenses (forcible rape, robbery, aggravated assault, willful homicide) are added, the number rises to 5,158.6 per 100,000 population or more than five persons in 100. So there is a distinct possibility that you, a neighbor, friend or relative will be the target of a criminal act in the coming months.

The figures are for *reported* crimes only. Although citizens are more willing to report crimes today, many crimes still go unreported through neglect or fear by the victims. Officials estimate that the actual crime rate could be three times as great as the reported rate.

REPORTED CRIMES, 1983
Seven Major Offenses

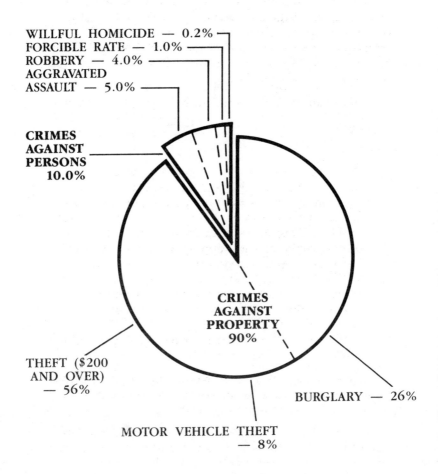

WILLFUL HOMICIDE — 0.2%
FORCIBLE RATE — 1.0%
ROBBERY — 4.0%
AGGRAVATED
ASSAULT — 5.0%

CRIMES
AGAINST
PERSONS
10.0%

CRIMES
AGAINST
PROPERTY
90%

THEFT ($200
AND OVER)
— 56%

BURGLARY — 26%

MOTOR VEHICLE THEFT
— 8%

Source: Federal Bureau of Investigation

NOTE: Statistics Rounded Off.

What types of crimes are committed? The chart on page 6. indicates crimes against property represent an astounding 90%, or 9 out of 10 reported crimes committed in the United States. Larceny — theft (shoplifting, pickpocketing, purse-snatching; thefts of bicycles, from coin machines, buildings and motor vehicles) are included in the crimes against property. Over a quarter (26%) of all crimes against property are burglaries. Robbery (theft by force) accounts for a much smaller percentage, about 4% of the seven major offenses.

Theft, in all its forms, is the most frequently committed crime, perhaps, as one law enforcement officer said, because it is so easy for the experienced to steal. Three out of four burglars arrested have prior convictions!

Statistical studies reveal some significant aspects of crime:
— Warm months are the peak season for personal and household crimes because people are away from home, outside and away on vacation more often.
— Residential burglaries occur most often during the day when people are out shopping, working or in school.
— Over 85% of all violent crimes occur away from the victim's homes, mostly on the street, parking lots, parks and inside nonresidential buildings.
— Highest crime rates are in very urban or resort areas; lowest in very rural areas.
— Pacific and Mountain states have the highest crime rates.

Thus, the chance of a crime happening to you depends a great deal on the type of crime, the month, the time of day and where you live.

Active participation by citizens in such programs as Operation I.D. and Neighborhood Watch and the general aging of America have significantly reduced total crime by 7% from 1982 to 1983. That is very encouraging for it means our efforts, alertness and prevention techniques do work. But, considering that over 12 million *reported* crimes occur in the United States every year, the risk is great and ever present.

CRIME CLOCK

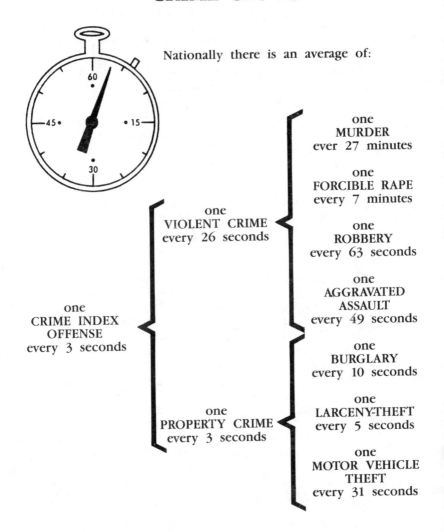

Nationally there is an average of:

one
VIOLENT CRIME
every 26 seconds

one
CRIME INDEX
OFFENSE
every 3 seconds

one
PROPERTY CRIME
every 3 seconds

one
MURDER
ever 27 minutes

one
FORCIBLE RAPE
every 7 minutes

one
ROBBERY
every 63 seconds

one
AGGRAVATED
ASSAULT
every 49 seconds

one
BURGLARY
every 10 seconds

one
LARCENY-THEFT
every 5 seconds

one
MOTOR VEHICLE
THEFT
every 31 seconds

Represents the annual ratio of crime
to fixed time intervals in 1983

Source: U.S. Department of Justice
        Federal Bureau of Investigation
        Crime In The United States

8.

Property theft, the most frequent crime, will still be with us in the future, too, as will the rising rates in homeowners, auto and other forms of theft insurance. A thief does not just steal from your neighbor or the family in the next town, he steals from each of us. He takes money out of our pockets to pay for the physical damage that must be repaired after the crime, to pay for the insurance we must buy to protect our property and to pay for the additional security measures we must have for ourselves and our community. These extended expenses are not often measured but they do exist.

From experience, individual citizen participation has become the best deterrent to crime. Studies reveal that the areas with low crime rates have strong locks and even stronger community bonds. Not only is it wise to secure your own home, but it's also a good idea to keep a neighborly watch over the apartments in your building or the homes in your neighborhood. It's no longer enough to rely solely on the overburdened police. Informed, prepared and alert citizens can reduce their risks of becoming the numbers in next year's crime reports.

CHAPTER 2

HOW YOUR LOCAL POLICE DEPARTMENT CAN HELP YOU

Citizen participation programs are an increasingly important part of police work. Many local police departments have a Crime Prevention Bureau to advise residents on crime prevention strategies. These experts have found that a resident's own preventative measures are the most effective.

The Crime Prevention Bureau is a valuable resource for specific questions or general aid in securing your home. The specialists in these Bureaus know which crimes are most frequently committed, the kinds of criminals operating in your area, and the best methods to take to thwart their activity.

The Bureaus usually offer these other services:

Block Meetings

At your request and by appointment, police officers will conduct a crime prevention meeting in a private home in your neighborhood. Neighbors on the same block are invited. During the course of the meeting, the police officers will explain the idea of block meetings and various aspects of burglary prevention, how burglars operate and how to evaluate and react to potentially dangerous situations. They will also explain how to use an engraving tool for personally identifying valuable property burglars are likely to steal. And, most importantly, they are there to answer your questions and discuss the block's common crime problems.

Neighborhood Watch

This citizen awareness program has significantly reduced crime in areas where it has been established. As an effective crime prevention program, Neighborhood Watch trains neighbors to be alert for potential criminal activity on their block. In regularly held Neighborhood Watch meetings, the crime prevention specialist will instruct neighbors to be on guard against suspicious, unfamiliar persons or vehicles in the neighborhood, unusual activity in and around a neighbor's house and how to report suspicions or events to the police. Neighbors are encouraged to call each other through a neighborhood relay calling system to check on each other's safety and to alert each other if there is an emergency. The Neighborhood Watch police specialist will also inform residents about any recent criminal activity in the neighborhood, teach the latest home crime prevention techniques and answer specific questions.

By getting to know each other while learning about crime prevention, neighbors become more concerned with safeguarding each other's property during the day and during vacations. Thus, when you're going to be away for an extended period of time, a trusted neighbor can be given a key to your residence so he or she can change the draperies' position, alternate lighting timers or asked to deposit their garbage in your empty cans and set them out on pickup day. (You can return the favor when your neighbor is going to be away.)

Neighborhood Watch promotes a sense of community between neighbors and concern about the safety of the neighborhood. By sharpening your and your neighbor's awareness of who belongs and who doesn't and knowing when and how to report suspicions to the proper authorities quickly, you are helping local police do a more efficient job of protecting you. Neighborhood Watch revitalizes old-fashioned neighborly spirit to help reduce the crime rate where you live.

For further information on setting up a Neighborhood Watch for your block or apartment building, contact the Crime Prevention Officer of your local police department or station.

WARNING!
THESE PREMISES
ARE PROTECTED
All contents have permanent
registered code marks
They can be traced
By Law Enforcement Agencies
Operation
HomeGuard

Free Home Security Checks

By appointment, a specially trained police officer will evaluate your home's security. Special or unusual problems can be pointed out and discussed at this time. Generally, there is no charge for this service, making it one of the most valuable resources in town.

Free Emergency Phone Stickers

These printed stickers easily affix to the front or top of the phone or receiver and, in an emergency, can be a life-saver. Dialing the operator in an emergency is not as fast or efficient as dialing directly the appropriate agency number of the police, fire, paramedics or ambulance or the new 911 all-purpose emergency number.

If your police department does not have these printed phone stickers, take a few minutes to write down your local emergency numbers on a small piece of paper and tape it to your phone. When seconds count, that little sticker becomes one of the most important preventative measures you will ever take.

Crime prevention is a tough job. There are so many criminals; so few police officers. With your interest and concern, your police department can more effectively protect you and yours. All it takes is a phone call to your local Crime Prevention Bureau for more information.

CHAPTER 3
WHO ARE THE CRIMINALS?

Movies would have us believe that most crimes are plotted long hours by clever crooks in careful detail. Rather, a thief, the most prevalent criminal, is really an opportunist who looks for an easy target, a quick snatch and a fast getaway. Usually young and male, he capitalizes on our carelessness, neglect or off-guard moments. The average burglar will cruise the streets looking for tell-tale signs of an unoccupied house — the lawn not watered, newspapers piled up or a mailbox stuffed with several days accumulation. The purse snatcher or robber looks for a vulnerable victim.

Other thieves are more devious. One type may drive a paneled truck and dress as a serviceman or inspector of some kind, gaining entry on the unsuspecting occupant. He then appraises the contents of the house for a worthwhile haul. Another type may try telephoning first to make certain the owner is not at home, using a pretext of a wrong number if the phone is answered. Or the thief may pose as a poll taker, asking questions about the family's habits, vacation plans or recent purchases.

Yet, there are other types of burglars that brazenly enter a house regardless of whether or not it is occupied. Most residents will not encounter such a person, but, if you are home during an attempted burglary, it's prudent to know what kind of person he is and how to deal with him.

Of course, each confrontation is different and you must rely on your best judgment as to how *you* will react. (See page 45., "If You're Home During A Burglary" for details.)

On the average, however, the common burglar wants no confrontation with his intended victim — just the loot. Knowing this, the wise occupant takes care that his dwelling looks lived-in and secure against a burglar's simple entry.

Some types of burglars are:

The Juveniles

Juveniles (under 18) accounted for almost 40% of all burglary arrests in the nation in 1983! The juvenile burglar is acting on impulse, scared and unpredictable. Above all, he does not want to be caught. So give him plenty of leeway to beat a hasty retreat and, chances are, he will.

The Professional

He has done some careful planning and research before he settles on his target. After casing a house, he comes prepared: gloves, mask, rubber-soled shoes. He is reasonable, calm, and assured. And he's planned his exit route as well. If he carries a weapon, he is especially dangerous; he will not flee so easily.

The Drug Addict

This burglar is looking for goods that will buy him his next fix and that makes him almost desperate. However, he does not want trouble and it's unlikely he will attack if discovered. But, if attacked, his reactions are very unpredictable and may be violent.

The Sex Attacker

He may only be a non-aggressive "Peeping Tom" who will quickly retreat — if he enters a house at all. On the other hand, the obsessive personality that propels a rapist to break in, even into a locked bedroom must be aggressively resisted. (The section on Rape deals more extensively with how to repel this kind of housebreaker.)

In summary, most burglars prefer an unoccupied residence for their work. Therefore, it is especially important that your home appears occupied even if no one is there.

CHAPTER 4
A HOME SECURITY PLAN

A secure residence is your first line of defense against intruders. Some proven recommendations to help burglar-proof your home:

LANDSCAPING

An unobstructed view of your house does not allow the burglar the privacy he needs to gain entry. Your neighbors and patrolling police can more easily spot any trespassers.

— Trim back any shrubbery or plant growth that blocks the view of your front door or windows from the street.
— Cut back any tree limbs that may provide easy access to a second story window.
— Trim hedges and other plant growth low, away from side and rear windows and doors.
— Mow and water lawns regularly.

LIGHTING

The more light — inside and outside — of your home, the better to discourage burglars.

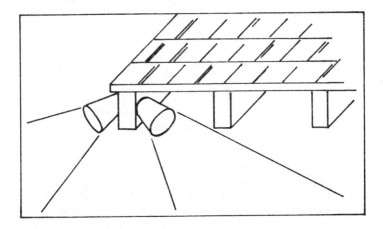

— Light all sides of the house: front, rear, sides.
— Place exterior floodlights below the eaves or edge of the roof for maximum effect. Wire coverings on outside lights protect against intentional bulb breakage.
— Hook up an automatic timer to your outside lights that will turn exterior lights on at dusk and off at dawn. A well-lit yard discourages night prowlers.

— "Burn a light at night" with inexpensive timers easily attached to inside lamps in one or more rooms and set to appropriate times to go on and off. If you will be away overnight, set the timer to switch off the lights about your bedtime so that the telltale signs of lights burning all night are not a give-away to the determined burglar. When you are returning home late at night, keep a lamp lit. It's safer to enter a lighted room than a dark one.

DOORS

Even the best doors and locks are of no use if you forget to close them tightly and lock them securely each time you leave your house, even if you're only working in the backyard. Of course, you should never open a door to a stranger until you are fully satisfied as to his purpose.

— Install a wide angle viewer with a one-way view to the outside. Then you can identify visitors *before* you open the door.
— All exterior doors should be of a solid core construction for greater security.

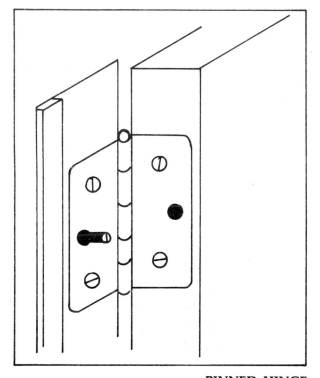

PINNED HINGE

— Pin hinge plates on exterior door. Remove one screw from the door side of the hinge and its opposite from the door frame hinge. Insert a solid metal pin screw or concrete nail in the screw's place on the door frame side. It should extend about 1/2 inch. Drill a hole on the opposite side to fit the pin. Repeat this process for each of the door's hinges. Then, the closed and locked door cannot be lifted even if the outside hinge pins are removed.

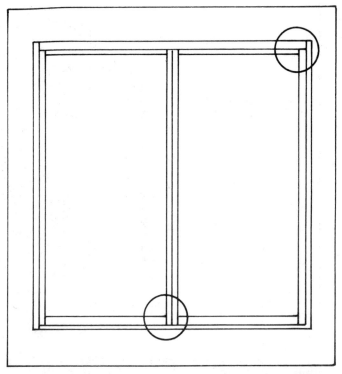

SLIDING DOOR

Sliding Glass Doors present special problems. There are a number of ways to prevent entry:

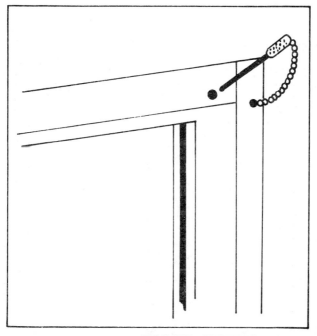

PINNED SLIDING PANEL

— Metal pins can be inserted into drilled holes in the
top channel through to the door frame. Attach the
pin to a cord or light chain and drop it through a
screw eye near the door for easy storage when not
in use.
— Metal or wooden rods (such as broomsticks) can be
placed in the lower channel to prevent a sliding door
from being pried open. Make sure the rod fits snugly
into the track when the door is closed.

SLIDE-BOLT

— Slide bolts, anti-slide blocks and other locks manufactured especially for sliding glass doors (and windows) are readily available.

ANTI-SLIDE BLOCK

SLIDE-BOLT

SLIDE-BOLT WITH PADLOCK

Keyed locking devices offer no absolute security and they can be a fire exit hazard.

Double Doors, especially with glass inserts, need additional protective devices.

   — Cane bolts are much better than weak, inadequate slide-bolts. Cane bolts are 1/2 inch in diameter and 12 inches high, installed at the top and bottom of the inactive door.

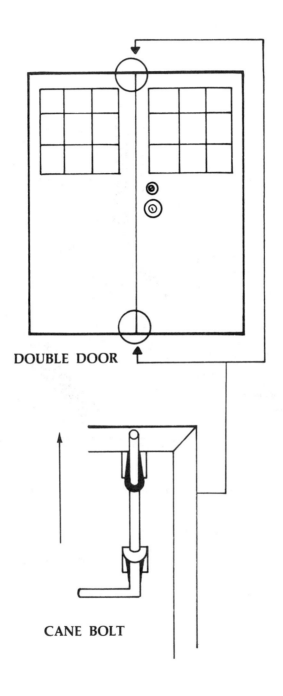

DOUBLE DOOR

CANE BOLT

— Flush bolts, fitted inside the top and bottom of the inactive door, are better since the intruder cannot get at them when the doors are locked.

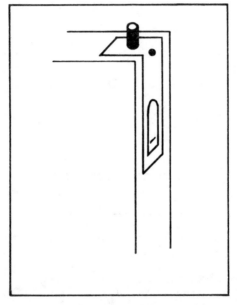

FLUSH BOLT

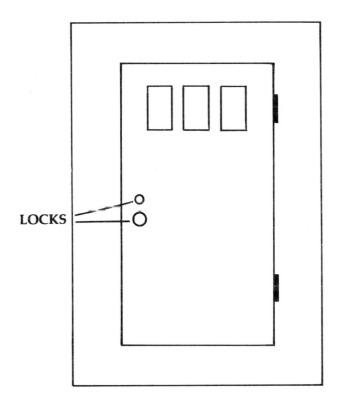

LOCKS

DOOR LOCKS

The cheapest insurance and the wisest investment a homeowner or apartment dweller can buy are sturdy locks. Your local hardware store or locksmith have a variety of these.

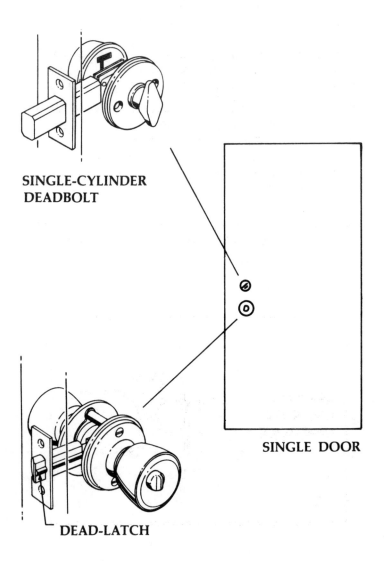

SINGLE-CYLINDER DEADBOLT

SINGLE DOOR

DEAD-LATCH

Dead latch is an inexpensive addition to an existing knob lock set. It prevents the burglar from simply slipping in a credit card to spring open the door.

Dead bolt locks are a better choice. A quality dead bolt lock should have at the very minimum:
— a one inch extension of the bolt
— a cylinder guard ring of hardened steel
— a hardened steel insert or bearing inside the bolt so it cannot be sawed off
— all screws of 1½″ length

If there is glass within 40 inches of the lock, a double cylinder one-inch deadbolt is recommended instead.

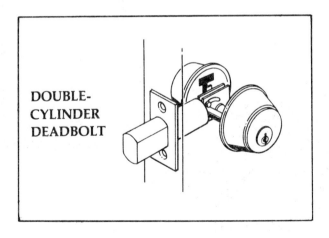

DOUBLE-CYLINDER DEADBOLT

Rim locks are one-inch deadbolts installed on the interior surface of the door and equally effective. "Jimmy proof" rim locks with vertical dead bolts offer an extra measure of security.

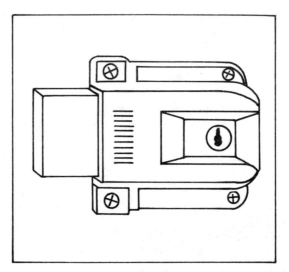

RIM LOCK

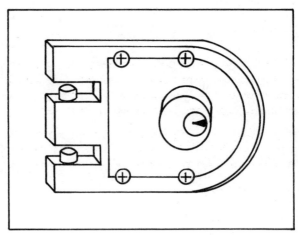

"JIMMY PROOF" RIM LOCK

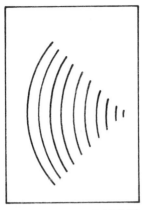

ALARMS

DOOR ALARMS

Exterior doors can be rigged to set off an alarm when opened without authorization. Portable door alarms are often recommended for apartment dwellers. One type looks like a transistor radio; it simply hangs on the doorknob and has an off-on switch. If someone tries your door during the night, it sets off a loud enough noise to wake you up, scare away the burglar and can even alert the neighbors.

A locksmith or specialty security store can suggest other types of door alarms appropriate for your purpose.

REMEMBER to install locks on all exterior doors, not just the front door. Outside doors and windows should always be locked even if you're only going down the street or running an errand for a few minutes. Lock doors and windows even when you are at home. Some burglars look for residents working in the yard, washing a car or engaged outside. Then they enter from the opposite side of the house to steal purses, money or other valuable items while the unsuspecting victim is nearby.

WINDOWS

Most burglars will not break a window for fear the noise will attract attention, but they will attempt to open one.

— Be sure windows are closed, securely fastened and the blinds drawn when guests are using a room for storing purses and jackets. Even a slightly open window will permit a thief to manipulate a long pole inside to pick up valuables.

— Where windows are frequently open, screens should be securely attached to their frames and the window moldings.

— Select the appropriate lock for each type of window in your home.

Louvre windows (notoriously the worst risks because the individual panes can be easily lifted out).

— Apply a two-part epoxy resin to each end of each pane. Inset back into each holder, or

— Install grilles or grates. In bedrooms, make sure the grates can be opened from the inside as a quick and safe fire exit, especially in children's and guest rooms, or

— Replace the louvres with solid glass or another type of window.

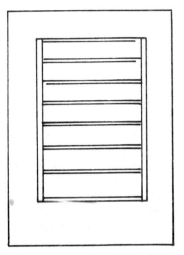

LOUVER WINDOW

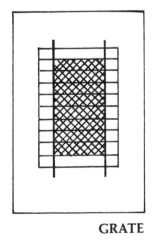

GRATE

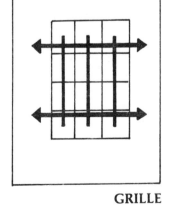

GRILLE

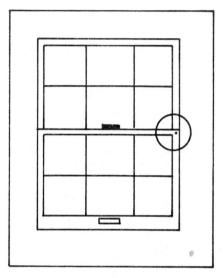

DOUBLE HUNG

Double Hung Sash A latch is not enough for it can be jimmied open. For windows that are used, drill a hole that angles slightly downward through a top corner of the bottom window into the bottom of the top window. Insert a solid pin or nail into the hole. If the sash window is not in a bedroom or never opened, install a keyed sash latch or screw the window shut.

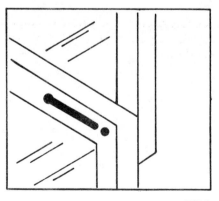

PIN

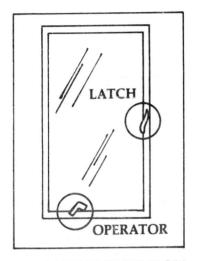

CASEMENT WINDOW

Casement crank windows are the easiest to secure. Make certain the locking latch works properly and that the crank which opens and closes it has no excess play. Replace any worn hardware.

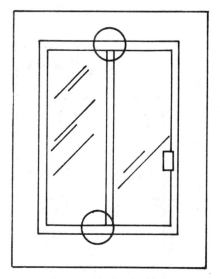

SLIDING WINDOW

Sliding glass windows should be secured in the same manner as sliding doors.

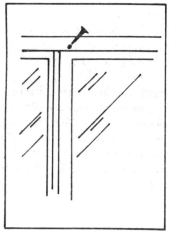

PINNED WINDOW

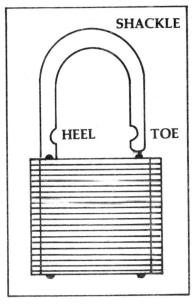

PADLOCK

GATES AND FENCES

Solidly built and well maintained gates and fences are further deterrents against illegal or unwanted entry. Buy and use quality padlocks that have:

- laminated or extruded cases,
- hardened steel shackle with a minimum diameter of 9/32 inch but heavier shackles offer better protection,
- double locking bolt for heel and toe locking,
- at least a 5 pin tumbler in the cylinder,
- key retaining feature which prevents removal of the key until the padlock is locked (as a reminder to lock the padlock).

GARAGES

An unlocked garage may have just the tools or ladder that the burglar needs to break into your house. Or, he may be in the market for the items you store in your garage.

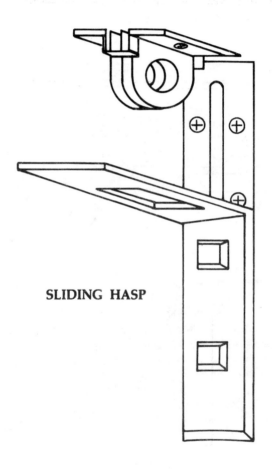

SLIDING HASP

— Use hardened steel hasps and padlocks to secure both sides of a lifting garage door. Deface the threads of the bolt end with a hammer to keep the nuts from being removed. Be sure to use sturdy exterior padlocks. Install a pair of cane bolts on the inside.
— Install deadbolt locks on walk-through doors.
— Secure garage windows in the same way as you did for the windows in your home. If garage windows are kept shut, use nails or screws to keep them permanently closed.

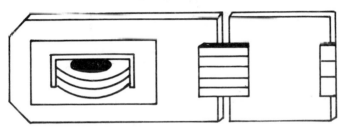

HANGING HASP

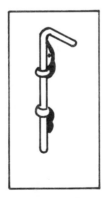

CANE BOLT

EXTERIOR STORAGE LOCKERS

Commonly used by apartment residents, exterior storage lockers are easily accessible to thieves.

- Use quality padlocks.
- Remove exposed hinges and install one-way, non-removable screws or interior hinges.

PET DOORS

A vulnerable point in your home's security, pet doors may be just the right size for a burglar to slip through or reach up and unlock the door from the inside. Secure the pet door with a sturdy lock and use it.

OTHER OPENINGS

Don't overlook ventilation openings, air-conditioning and heating ducts, crawl spaces, skylights and grilles. Heavy duty, well-attached screenings or locks will deter entry through these points.

RESIDENTIAL SECURITY SYSTEMS

Today's sophisticated burglar alarm systems have a variety of features designed to help burglar-proof your house electronically, ranging from do-it-yourself kits to silent alarms wired to the company's central station, the police or private patrol service.

If you're in the market for one, shop and compare, get the advice and services of a reputable company and buy only the features you need. Minimum features of a good system are:

- a battery fail-safe back up,
- fire sensing capability,
- read-out ability to check the workings of the system,
- horn sounding device installed in attic through vents.

Remember, *don't* rely solely on an alarm system. It is no substitute for installing and using sturdy locking devices.

DOGS

A best friend in more ways than one, the family pooch need not be a trained attack dog; the best kind has the loudest bark. However, considering the expense and upkeep of a dog, obtaining one just as a burglar deterrent is probably not a good idea. Smart burglars carry chemical sprays or use other methods to quiet them down. And, if you're going away, the dog will either go with you or be boarded elsewhere. Finally, a dog cannot take the place of solid doors and strong locks. On the other hand, if you're going to get a dog for other reasons anyway, a convincing barker is a good choice.

NEW DWELLINGS
When you move into a new dwelling — be it a larger home, an apartment, condominium, mobile home park, or retirement village — consider new locks as part of your moving expenses and install them *before* you move in. A reputable locksmith can either change the keying of the present locks or, if the present locks are inadequate, replace them with the stronger ones. Change locks....

— Even if the previous owner has left all the keys. You do not know whether other persons have had access to them and have had duplicate ones made.
— Even if it's a brand new residence. Numerous workmen may have had keys to your home during construction or the builder might still have a master key to all the units.

With your own upgraded locks installed, you'll sleep better in your new surroundings.

SAFE PLACES INSIDE YOUR HOME
The burglar's favorite place for finding jewelry, cash, credit cards and other valuables is anywhere in the master bedroom — and they aren't hesitant about looking underneath the lingerie and in home office desks. Don't tape combination lock numbers in the inside middle desk drawer or leave keys there.

Security Closets
Establish a security closet for cameras, furs, guns and silver. Choose a closet in the middle of a wall with no exposed sidewalls.

— Line with fire resistant gypsum board.
— Install at least a one inch deadbolt or two drop bolt locks, one placed six inches above the original lock, the other, six inches below.
— Hide the key safely, far away from the location of the door.
— Pin the door hinges or flatten the hinge pins so the door cannot be removed.
— Reinforce the door itself with plywood on the inside or steel on the outside.

"Traps"

Hidden boxes may be built inside a piece of furniture.

Home Safes

While no substitute for a safe deposit box for papers and small valuables, home safes should weigh at least 200 pounds and be fire resistant, but don't expect it to keep out expert safecrackers. Best location is embedded in a concrete basement wall or floor.

IF YOU DISCOVER A BREAK-IN

Always take a few seconds as you approach your house to observe any strange vehicles, especially unexpected paneled trucks parked in front, opened or broken windows and any change in the interior or exterior lighting than when you left. If you find these changes, *do not* attempt to enter. Instead, note the description and license number of the suspicious vehicle and use a neighbor's phone to call police. Even if it turns out to be a false alarm, at least you have not placed yourself or your family in danger.

In the unhappy event you find your dwelling ransacked, do not touch anything. Just leave everything as it is and call the police immediately. Supply the officers with the necessary information. On arrival, they will look for the point of entry and take fingerprints. Have serial numbers and descriptions ready for any missing items. (See page 73.) If you find more articles missing later, be sure to call and add them to the report.

IF YOU'RE HOME DURING A BURGLARY

Awakened from sleep late at night by unfamiliar noises? Proceed with extreme caution and use your best judgment. If you can, quietly call the police. Give them such information as your location in the house and license number of any strange vehicle parked outside. If your telephone line has been cut, lock your bedroom door, open a window and scream "FIRE" as loudly as possible. It might attract a neighbor's or passerby's attention or, best of all, scare off the intruder. Turning on the radio full blast and creating other kinds of noise help too.

Crime prevention experts recommend several courses of action if you are confronted by a burglar, but each one requires advance planning:

— Make the master bedroom a "security room"; that is, prepare this room for emergency as well as its customary use. Install a sturdy lock on the inside of the master bedroom door.

— Place a telephone, flashlight and some kind of loud noise-maker on or near the nightstand. A radio, a small mariner's airhorn (readily available at marine supply stores) or police-type whistle create enough sound that could scare off the burglar and attract aid.

— An aerosol can of hair spray, cover removed and on the nightstand, makes a handy weapon for self-defense in the improbable event that all of the above have failed. Sprayed directly at the attacker's face, it will create time for you to flee. However, this method presupposes enough light and presence of mind to react quickly and effectively.

— Teargas or Mace must be used knowledgeably. These toxic sprays temporarily burn and blind assailants. Some states require formal classroom training and certification by local law enforcement agencies before the spray can be purchased. Your local police department will have specific information.

— Home guns present special moral and legal problems and responsibilities. Tragically, many more sleepwalking family members are shot per year than burglars. And, there's always the possibility, in any confrontation, that the gun can be taken away and used against you. Crooks like stolen guns because they cannot be traced back to them. For these reasons and others, police generally discourage home guns. Better a loss of property than a loss of life.

VACATION CHECKLIST

Burglars look for absentee residences to invade. Use this checklist to make sure your vacation includes peace of mind about the security of your house back home:

- ☐ No announcements in even local papers about your upcoming plans.
- ☐ Car packing done in garage or out of sight. Cruising burglars will notice who is loading a car with suitcases and come back later.
- ☐ Discontinue all deliveries: mail, newspaper, milk, etc. Arrange for the post office to hold or forward your mail.
- ☐ Ask a trusted neighbor to pick-up throwaways, advertising circulars, debris and notes left on your door, to report any suspicious persons or unusual activity near your home, to change position of drapes or window blinds from time to time. (You can return the favor when it's time for his vacation.)
- ☐ Attach timers to exterior and interior lights.
- ☐ Notify Police Department and a neighbor as to your departure and return, lighting arrangements and where you can be reached. Special police watches can be provided.
- ☐ Arrange to have lawns watered and shrubbery trimmed.
- ☐ Turn telephone bell down to its lowest level and muffle with a towel. A ringing telephone is a clue you are not home.
- ☐ Yard gates securely padlocked.
- ☐ Tools, ladder are locked up in a secured garage.
- ☐ Windows and doors locked.

Be sure to notify police upon your return.

HOUSESITTERS FOR EXTENDED ABSENCES

For a lengthy trip away from home, a good burglary deterrent is a friend, a relative, co-worker, or someone you know well to housesit, but check references thoroughly if appropriate.

Spend a few hours before you leave acquainting the person with the security measures of your home. Go over the operation of any alarm systems, emergency numbers, and the household routine (gardeners, pool service). Have the housesitter meet the neighbors so they can become familiar with his routine and he with theirs.

One of the advantages of a housesitter is that your dog will be able to remain home, guarding your property as well. Be sure the housesitter is agreeable to caring for the dog too.

CHAPTER **5**
HOME FIRE PREVENTION
... AND HOTEL FIRE SAFETY

As the third largest accidental killer in the nation (ranking after motor vehicles and falls and before drownings), fire is a special danger in residences. Over 80% of all deaths from fire occur where people sleep: homes, apartments, hotels, motels and mobile homes.

A brief look at the statistics, as reported by the National Fire Protection Association, indicates the nature of fire danger:

— About 8 out of 10 residential fire deaths occur in one and two family dwellings.

— Almost $6.5 million property damage over-all.

— The largest and smallest communities had the highest fire incident rates.

— The Northeast and Southeast regions experienced the highest incident rate of fire and fire-caused deaths.

— About two-thirds of all residential fire deaths occur between 8 p.m. and 8 a.m. and start in living rooms, bedrooms and kitchens.

— Fire from smoldering cigarettes in upholstery and bedding is the most common cause of fire deaths.

The warning is clear: the common home fire is the most likely to happen to you and your family.

Let's take a closer look at the nature of fire and some basic common sense measures to protect your life and property.

The Nature of Fire

Fire is a combination of three elements: fuel, air and heat. Quite simply, keeping each of these elements apart prevents fire. That's why it is especially important to keep all fuel sources including combustibles and flammable liquids far removed from any possible heat sources. Vapors emitting from flammable solvents, when mixed with air in certain proportions, can be readily ignited.

Another significant fact about fire is that flames themselves do not account for the bulk of fire fatalities. Rather, it's suffocation from the toxic, superheated gases and inhaled smoke released by the flames that causes fire deaths. Smoke and fire gases rise quickly up stairwells and wall cavities. Generally, smoke alone will not awaken sleeping persons. Instead, the inhaled smoke puts them into a deeper sleep, eventually causing death. Since so many deaths occur when victims were sleeping in upper story bedrooms, these rooms are especially vulnerable.

How To Safeguard Against the Major Causes of Fire
Most home fires originate from five common sources. But in reality there is only one chief cause — human carelessness. If we can correct that fault, we've gone a long way towards reducing the risk of fire in our homes.

1. *Careless Smoking and Matches* Smoking and careless use of matches are the most significant cause of home fires and the chief cause of fire deaths. A few precautions taken with family and guests in your home will cut down this threat.

— Never smoke in bed. *Never* allow ashtrays or smoking in bedrooms. The chance of drifting off to sleep with a burning cigarette in hand is just too great. For the same reason, if you're smoking in a comfortable chair and feel drowsy, put it out right then.

— Provide large, deep ashtrays for smokers to prevent lighted cigarettes, pipes or cigars from falling out undetected. Lighted smokes can easily drop into upholstery and smolder for hours before bursting into flames.

— Be especially alert if you or your guests drink *and* smoke. Then, it's too easy to become forgetful about handling a cigarette carefully. Alcohol also reduces reaction time to a developing fire and, if you have been drinking, makes you less likely to hear a smoke detector when sleeping.

— Before emptying ash trays, check the contents carefully to make sure cigarettes and ashes are cold. Flush butts in the toilet.

— Before retiring for the night, if there are or have been smokers in your house, check all rooms to make sure no one has left a cigarette, cigar or pipe burning.

— Matches and lighters present additional hazards, especially with children around. Keep them safely stored in high places in a metal box away from curious little fingers.

— Never use matches or candles to light attics, closets or dark corners. Have a flashlight handy instead.

— Get into the habit of breaking matches and checking the tips before discarding them. Teach older children match safety.

— Never leave matches stored in pockets of clothing.

2. *Heating Equipment* When the temperature outside goes down, we turn the heat up or light the fireplace. Yet defective, improperly installed or operated and poorly maintained heating equipment accounts for many home fires.

— Check *heating systems* each year preferably by a professional in the fall before seasonal demands place a heavy strain on inadequate equipment. Follow regular cleaning and maintenance schedules listed by the manufacturer, but do not try to repair or replace parts yourself unless you also happen to be a professional. Have the repairman check walls and ceiling near the furnace and install additional insulation if necessary. Check fuel pipes to see if they are well supported, clean and free of holes. A good suggestion would be to install a safety shut-off switch for a basement heater at the top of the stairs. If you smell gas or oil, turn the heater off and close the basement door tightly. Evacuate the house until the leak is located and professionally repaired.

Make sure trash and combustibles are kept far away from the heating system and that the area is clean.

— *Fireplaces* should have a large metal protective screen. Start fireplace fires cautiously but never with gasoline or other fuels. Rugs and furniture belong at least three feet away from the actual fire. Flimsy or flammable objects should not be placed on the mantlepiece above the fire. Do not use the fireplace or space heaters to dry clothes. When you leave the house or go to bed, make sure all sparks and embers are extinguished. Chimney spark arresters and dampers need to be checked yearly, preferably by professional chimney sweeps. Remove creosote which builds up in the fireplace and is very flammable. Chimney cracks and loose bricks should be repaired. Seal unused flue openings with solid masonry.

— *Room heaters* need thorough checking and cleaning too. Place them where they will not be bumped or overturned accidentally or block emergency fire exits. A safety screen around heater prevents contact especially by children. Ventilate home heaters adequately by placing them a safe distance from walls, clothes racks, curtains, furniture and beds. Follow manufacturer's directions for proper venting. Electrical heaters need adequate wiring to carry the extra load. Use the proper grade of kerosene. Never mix gasoline with fuel and never use a gasoline can for fuel oil or kerosene. Oil units should not be filled while burning nor overfilled. At bedtime, turn off room heaters or set on "low" and, if it's in a bedroom, open a window to prevent possible suffocation.

3. *Electrical Equipment and Circuits*
Beware the danger signs:
- frequently blown fuses or circuit breakers,
- faulty switches,
- frayed cords,
- wires strung under rugs or nailed or stapled to walls,
- inadequate wirings for Christmas, holiday and party decorations.

Unless you are a qualified electrician, have a professional check your home's wiring system and make needed updating. Yesterday's wiring is not sufficient for today's demands.

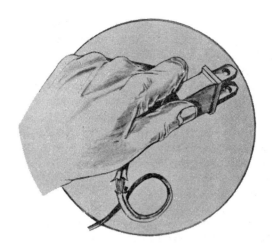

Rewiring is not a job for an otherwise handy person. The electrician will also know your community's electrical code and safe materials to use. It's money well spent to modernize your house's electrical system; a fire can cost you a lot more.

— Make sure television cabinets are placed far enough away from the wall for adequate ventilation. TVs in recessed, wall or home-made cabinets need sufficient breathing space too. Vacuum the TV regularly to remove lint and dust on wires and tubes.

— Outside TV antennas need proper grounding to prevent lightning damage. The antenna should be so installed that it cannot fall across powerlines, damage your chimney or cause a fire.

— Disconnect all electrical appliances when not in use, including TVs, especially the instant-on types. Irons, toasters, coffeemakers, blenders and other small electrical appliances should not be left plugged in.

— Use extension cords sparingly and check for cracks in the cord each time.

— If you use power tools, check that your workshop or garage has enough electrical capacity to provide adequate current.

— Buy and use only UL (Underwriters Laboratories) approved electrical products and appliances.

— Teach your family how to operate the master electric switch. If an electrical fire should start, they'll know how to shut-off the master switch immediately.

4. *Cooking Equipment* A kitchen is a room full of potential fire hazards, and the scene of numerous home accidents. Don't give a kitchen fire a chance to start.

— Keep the stove free from accumulated grease. Daily cleaning is a kind of fire prevention insurance. Check grease build-up and clean vents, hoods and indoor barbecues regularly.

— Keep grease cans, matches, dishes, clothes and aerosol cans away from the stove.

— Flammable objects such as clothing, dish towels, pot holders and paper goods should never be hung nor dried near the burners.

— Never store children's treats over the stove or cooktop. Burners could be accidentally turned on or still hot from use when children climb up to reach a favorite goodie.

— If your kitchen range is located underneath a window, secure kitchen curtains at least three feet away so that they cannot blow over the burners.

— Don't leave food cooking on stove unattended.

— If you smell gas, call the gas company immediately.

— Keep handles of pots and pans turned toward the center of the stove so that they cannot accidentally be knocked over, and are out of reach of young children in the house.

— Avoid wearing loose clothing or long sleeves when working at the stove.

— Thoroughly vacuum the sides and underneath stoves, refrigerators and freezers every six months.

Grease fires are the most common types of kitchen fires. If grease flares up inside the oven, close the oven door and turn off the oven heat. If that does not work slip a metal lid over the container to smother the flame or sprinkle baking powder or salt over it. Never use water or flour. Use the same techniques for pan fires on top of the stove. Call the fire department without delay if these efforts fail.

5. *Flammable Liquids* The best prevention for eliminating flammable liquid fire is not to store them in the house or garage at all. Not only is the flammable liquid a danger, but the vapors themselves are combustible under certain conditions. Also, there's always the chance that a spark or open flame (such as from a water heater or gas dryer) will set it off and such fires can spread rapidly.

- Never, under any condition, store such flammables in the house. If you must use them, keep them safely stored in the garage or shed in clean metal containers. If flammable liquids are bought in other than metal containers, transfer the liquids into metal cans with tightly fitting covers or approved containers before bringing them into the home. Do this out of doors.
- If you must use flammable liquids indoors, open enough doors and windows for cross ventilation to carry away the explosive fumes or, if that is not adequate, use an electric fan. Make sure there are no electrical heating units, pilot lights or other flames to ignite these low flash-point fumes.
- Never smoke when working with flammable liquids.
- Never use such liquids as gasoline, kerosene or turpentine to help start, restart or hurry up a fire.
- Read the manufacturer's warning on all flammable liquid cans carefully and heed the advice when disposing of them. Never throw them into a fire. This is also sound advice for disposing of common household aerosol cans such as deodorants and hair spray. *Never* toss them into an incinerator. If the cap is on, the contents can cause the can to explode and the heated fumes to burn.
- Spray paint, lacquer and insecticide cans should be used far removed from any possible heat source, motors and electrical tools. Store them away from direct sunlight.

— Keep work areas clean. If you're a hobbyist working with wood, be sure to sweep up the day's dust and shavings carefully and dispose of them properly. Even the dust kicked up by using an electric sander on certain woods can be explosive. Do not smoke as you work.
— Oily rags heaped in a corner can cause fire by spontaneous combustion. Keep them stored in heavy metal containers with tight lids for disposal later.
— On driveways, gasoline and oil drips from any type of motor vehicles should be promptly washed away with soap, water and a stiff brush. Even sparks from a falling wrench can ignite a fire from these drippings.
— Wax or oil mops should be stored in cool, well ventilated spots away from heating pipes, closely confined spaces and direct sunlight.

Also, beware of other sources of fire:
— Attic, garage, closets or basements. Periodically clean out these areas, especially of old newspapers, books, rags and leaves. Dispose of them properly.
— Incinerators. If your community allows open burning, use an approved incinerator located at a safe distance away from the house. Burn only on windless days to prevent sparks from flying. Check to see that embers are thoroughly extinguished when you are finished.
— Lightning. Fire from lightning is not a major threat in heavily populated areas because tall buildings and water towers will divert it. However, in unprotected, isolated, open or elevated areas, special precautions are needed. Install lightning rods for residences in such areas to safely ground direct lightning or "side-flashes" from nearby trees.

FIRE SAFETY PLANNING

If fire breaks out in your home tonight, would you or your family know how to escape? Is there fire fighting equipment or, better yet, fire and smoke warning devices installed in your home?

Take the time to *equip* your house and *train* your family for this emergency. Forewarned is forearmed.

SMOKE DETECTORS

Smoke detectors have proved so effective in warning of fire's early stages that many cities require them installed in all homes and buildings. The Federal government requires them in all mobile homes. Insurance companies offer discounts on home fire insurance policies for smoke detectors in dwellings. One university research group found that out of 1200 fire death cases, 59% would still be alive had their homes been protected by smoke detectors.

Government, research and business agree: no place where people sleep should be without at least one.

Smoke detectors are a necessity on every level of your dwelling. They are the cheapest fire insurance you can buy.

Types of Smoke Detectors

Basically, smoke detectors are designed to trigger a buzzerlike device when its sensing chamber detects smoke. The smoke detectors come in three types: photoelectric and ionization and a combination of the two. Photoelectric and ionization have different characteristics and respond according to the origin of the fire that produces the smoke.

— Photoelectric models, because of their construction have been found to respond faster to smoldering fires, such as those from lighted cigarettes dropped into upholstered furniture or bedding.

— Ionization models respond quickest to ''clean burning'' fires from paper, cloth or wood and other open flame types of fire.

However, all smoke detectors do eventually sound the alarm for all types of fires. But, when minutes count in saving lives, the photoelectric does a better job of detecting a smoldering fire sooner, important when people are sleeping, and with fewer false alarms. Consumer Guide® after exhaustive testing, recommends one of each type in your house for all around protection.

Both photoelectric and ionization smoke detectors come in battery, plug-in and hard wire models. Battery models give a distinctive warning noise when it's time to replace the battery, usually once a year. Plug-in models usually rely on household current (which may be disrupted if there's an electrical fire or power failure) and must be installed near an outlet (which may not be the best location). Hard wire units must be wired directly into the house wiring. Again, Consumer Guide® suggests one of each kind for total fire protection.

Which one should you buy? Because each person's needs and residence vary greatly and with well over 100 models on the market, it's best to check your local library's consumer guides or your local fire department for brand recommendations.

Whichever brand of smoke detector you choose, carefully read and follow the manufacturer's instructions for installation, location, maintenance and testing.

Placing Smoke Detectors

Because most fatal home fires are apt to take place when the family is asleep, it's imperative to strategically mount smoke detectors where they can be easily heard.

Because smoke rises, the exact center of a flat ceiling is the best location for a smoke detector. Minimum distance from each wall is 12 inches. For odd-shaped ceilings, a smoke detector should be placed one foot or more below the peak of an A-frame ceiling, and, on a beamed ceiling, installed on a centrally located beam itself and not between beams. In multi-storied houses, place a smoke detector at the center of the ceiling directly above the stairway and one in each upper level sleeping area.

Although sometimes necessary, wall mounts are not recommended, especially if you plan only one smoke detector.

If you must mount your smoke detector on an outside wall, such as in a mobile home, or if the ceiling is under a flat roof, with no attic, the top of any smoke detector should be placed on the wall at least 4 inches below the ceiling line, and no further than 12 inches below. Make sure the roof or wall is fully insulated to avoid thermal barrier. Otherwise, choose an interior wall to place your smoke detector.

Smoke detectors should be placed at least three feet away from heating and/or air conditioning registers. The heat and cold air movements in a house could draw the smoke completely away or dilute the smoke and delay the alarms. Place them away from fireplaces and bathrooms.

For average dwellings, place your smoke alarms:
— On the hallway ceiling within 15 feet of each bedroom door. If it's a long hallway or bedrooms are far apart, you'll need more than one. Ionization models are recommended here if they are not placed too close to a kitchen.
— On the ceiling of each bedroom in which a smoker sleeps. Photoelectric models work well for the possibility of a smoldering fire here.
— In multi-level homes, install one on each living level, and one in the stairwell.
— In family rooms, dens and recreation rooms or wherever a television set is, but not near fireplaces.
— In basements where furnaces and hot water heaters are located.

After installing smoke detectors, test each one to make sure it can be heard from the bedrooms. If the smoke detector can't be heard from the bedrooms or if the house is especially large, have an interconnecting hook-up so that one alarm will automatically trigger the others.

Testing and Maintenance

In purchasing your smoke alarm, make sure testing devices are easy to reach and simple to operate. Otherwise, if it's troublesome, you tend not to do it. Battery models will require an annual battery replacement but don't buy a supply. A fresh battery will last the expected lifetime.

— Test them once a month.
— To prevent dust build-up which may clog the alarm, vacuum them monthly as part of regular maintenance procedure.

Consult the manufacturer's instruction book for additional information.

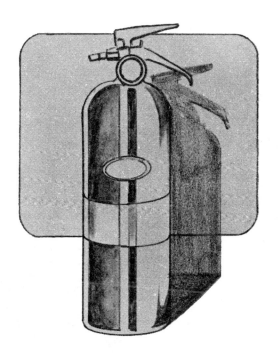

FIRE EXTINGUISHERS

If you discover a small fire in your home:

1. Get everyone out of the house *first*.
2. Call the fire department immediately.
3. Only then, if the fire is small, should you try to extinguish it while waiting for the fire department to arrive. Do not attempt to put out even a small fire unless you are certain you can fight it effectively and exit quickly.

Home extinguishers are a good idea to have around the house for controlling those unexpected small fires that could take a heavy toll of property damage. However, all fires are not alike and there are several types of fire extinguishers especially designed to fight particular classes of fires. This chart summarizes extinguishers available for home use:

Class	Fire Occurs In	Usual Home Location	Fire Extinguisher
A	rubbish, combustible materials, paper, cloth, and many plastics	living room, family room, den, bedroom, basement	water or multi-purpose dry chemical
B	flammable liquids, vapors, grease, paints, solvents	kitchen, utility room, workshop, laundry room, furnace, garage	standard dry chemical, purple K dry chemical, multi-purpose dry chemical or carbon dioxide (CO_2)
C	electrical appliances and equipment, faulty wiring	kitchen, workshop, garage, basement, TV room, bedroom	standard dry chemical, purple K dry chemical, multi-purpose dry chemical or carbon dioxide (CO_2)

Note: Only the multi-purpose dry chemical fights all three classes of fires. All three types of chemical sprays may leave a residue on the sprayed material. It must be cleaned up immediately after the fire is extinguished to lessen any damage caused by the chemical change. Carbon dioxide from those extinguishers dissipates as a harmless gas.

Shopping For A Fire Extinguisher

You can buy fire extinguishers designed for each specific class of fire, a multi-purpose fire extinguisher or a combination of the two.

In addition to the A, B, and/or C ratings on fire extinguisher labels, there will also be a numerical code in front of the letter. The numerical ratings indicate the ability of the extinguisher to put out the fire. Numbers start at 1 and increase in whole numbers. Thus, an extinguisher with a 10 B:C on its label will extinguish a class B or C fire twice the size as a 5 B:C rating. Class C fire extinguishers do not carry numerical codes; its only requirement is that it contain a fire stopping agent that does not conduct electricity.

Some fire extinguishers carry multiple numerical codes as well as letter codes. Thus a 2-A10-B:C code means the extinguisher will put out any class A, B or C fire of the size that might be safe for you to attempt to combat in your home.

To help you select the size of a fire extinguisher capability, the minimum protection that should be on your fire extinguisher for the area in which a fire is likely to occur is:

Class of Fire	Minimum Recommended Rating
all purpose A:B:C	2-A; 10-B:C
A	2-A
B & C	5-B:C

Fire extinguisher ratings are established by Underwriters Laboratories. Buy only a fire extinguisher that is Underwriters Laboratory approved or listed. It should be clearly marked on the label.

In addition to the Underwriters Laboratory listing, the label should contain the following information clearly stated:

1. operating instructions;
2. what to do after it has been used (i.e., how to recharge it);
3. how it should be maintained, tested and inspected;
4. letter and number rating.

As with smoke detectors, your local library has consumer guides to help you in selecting a brand of fire extinguisher to purchase or you may consult your local fire department for advice.

Location of Fire Extinguisher

Buy as many fire extinguishers as you think you'll need for your particular lifestyle. For example, a home hobbyist with a workshop in the garage should certainly have one there. Whatever you decide, match the types of extinguishers to the class of fire hazard likely to be encountered. Fire extinguishers should be installed in plain view, be easy to get to, and near a room exit that provides an escape route. Locate it away from potential fire hazards (the stove, TV, paint shelf). Otherwise, should a fire start there, it will be useless. If you don't plan to mount the unit on a wall, remove the mounting brackets to avoid impediments when you have to use it and, of course, keep it out of reach of children.

Use and Maintenance

The owner's manual will explain how to use the fire extinguisher you have purchased. Read the operating instructions carefully. Generally, to fight most home fires, keep 6 to 10 feet away from the fire and aim at the *base* of the flames. Use a side to side sweeping motion and stay low to the ground to avoid the rising smoke. Never let the fire get between you and the door exit. If it's an electrical fire, turn off the house current first. For a fire fed by a gas leak, shut off the gas at the main valve. If a fire extinguisher is used, gases may accumulate undetected presenting the real danger of explosion and rekindling of the fire. Again, do not attempt to fight any fire until everyone is out of the area and the fire department has been called.

Fire extinguisher units vary greatly in how and when they should be tested so, for dependable protection, follow maintenance schedules promptly such as an annual recharge and a 5 year hydrostatic test. Also, after using the fire extinguisher, follow directions carefully for putting in a replacement unit, recharging it or disposing of it.

Additional kinds of fire extinguishers are available for your car, your boat or particular home needs. Consult the telephone directory for authorized fire extinguisher services or talk to your local fire department for expert advice.

FIRE ESCAPE PLAN

Nighttime fires, the most deadly of home fires, cause blinding, lung-searing smoke and dangerous fumes, leaving little time to think clearly. With a plan, training and practice drills, each member of your household will know the most effective means to escape and safety.

— *Make Bedroom Surveys* Check that each bedroom has two escape routes in case one is cut off by flames or smoke. Choose a doorway and a window. Make sure windows *and* screens are easy to operate, open and get through from the inside. Keyed locks and stationary grilles should never be installed in bedroom windows. If necessary, rearrange the furniture in the room so that neither the doorway nor window exits are blocked. If windows are high and difficult to reach, place the bed or other climbing piece under the window.

For second story bedrooms, purchase or make an *escape ladder* and attach it securely inside the bedroom so that it is readily accessible and easily dropped. Test it to make sure it will hold the heaviest person in your house and the length reaches down far enough to the ground.

— *Make a Bedroom Floor Plan* Sketch the room's furnishings and mark the two selected escape routes.

Show the normal escape route, usually through a door. Mark the emergency exit in red. Post the floor plan on the back of the bedroom or closet door as a tangible reminder to its occupants. Point out these escape plans to babysitters and overnight guests in your home.

—*Teach Your Family* In a short family discussion, go through these steps for a fire escape procedure:
1. Keep bedroom doors closed at night. If you have smoke detectors outside bedroom doors, have the door slightly ajar. Ideally, you should have a smoke detector in each bedroom and sleep with door closed.
2. On awakening to an alarm, roll out of bed onto the floor and crawl under the smoke.
3. Agree on how to wake up sleeping family members in case fire cuts off the doorway. Whistles, horns, poundings on the walls and familiarity with the smoke detector's warning sound are some ways to do this.
4. "Everyone Out First." Don't waste precious time getting dressed, gathering valuables or checking on the source of the fire. Don't stop to rescue pets if it will endanger your life.
5. Decide on who will be responsible and how rescue will be accomplished for infants, elderly, handicapped or infirm residents of the house. Children need special instructions *not* to hide in closets or under beds.

6. Test doors before opening them. Before exiting through a door, feel the upper portion for heat and check for smoke leaking through the edges. If these conditions exist, use the alternate escape route.

   If you think the door is safe to open, do so cautiously by bracing your knee and shoulder behind the door and with one hand extended to feel for heat. Be ready to slam the door shut if smoke or heat rushes in. Again, use the emergency exit. If it is safe to exit, stay close to the floor where air is less smokey.

7. Decide on a prearranged outside meeting place to make sure everyone is safe and stay there. Do not attempt to reenter the house for whatever reason.

8. After everyone is accounted for, quickly call the fire department from a street alarm box or neighbor's phone. Speak clearly, giving your name and address. In an apartment building, give your name, address, the floor and apartment number where the fire is located.

   Wait for any questions or instructions. If you live in an isolated area, make advance arrangements with the local fire department on how to call them.

Special Note: If you live in a *multiple family residence* or work in a *high rise building,* your fire escape plan should be worked out not only for your own apartment or office area but for the building's escape routes as well. Know where the exit stairs are and what kind of fire alarm systems exist in the building, both for warning residents and for calling the fire department. Follow the general fire escape recommendations as for a house: feel for hot doors, stay low and near walls, open or break windows for ventilation. Above all, remain calm and follow the firefighters' instructions. If you become trapped, hang a large cloth such as a shirt or sheet out the window as a signal for rescue. If it becomes necessary use duct tape to seal the door from smoke. Remember, a closed door is a barrier to the spread of fire.

Hold Fire Drills

Hold two family fire drills to firmly fix these procedures in everyone's mind every six months: once, using the doorway as the exit; the second, using the emergency exits.

Special aids to infants and the infirm should also be practiced. Have everyone meet and be accounted for at your prearranged spot.

Remember, smoke rises. In an actual fire, you'd stay low to the floor or crawl and take short, shallow breaths. Deep gulps of heated air can be fatal. Break a window for more oxygen. Shut the door behind you and stay close to walls when going down stairs.

HOTEL FIRE SAFETY

Travel plans should include knowing how to protect yourself from fire in unfamiliar hotels and motels. Keep in mind, that, as in a home fire, the greatest danger is the smoke. At the first sign or scent of smoke, your main objective should be to get out of the hotel quickly and safely.

Before You Leave Home

When making hotel reservations, ask about the hotel's fire defense systems. Does it have a sprinkler system and a smoke detector in each room? Does it have a fire safety plan? Since most aerial ladders reach only to the eighth or tenth floor, request a room below the ninth floor in high rise hotel buildings.

To Take Along

Pack a portable smoke detector, battery radio, a flash-light and fresh batteries and a roll of duct tape. Smoke detectors now come in travel sizes that easily attach to top of hotel room or closet doors. Allow at least six inches below the ceiling and the smoke detector. If the ceiling is too low, it can be placed on the top of the tallest dresser or hung on a coat hanger and suspended from a hook or light fixture. Remember, do not place in corners of rooms.

On Arrival At The Room

Follow these procedures *before* you unpack or rest As one fire official put it, "You may never have the chance to gather this information again!"

Make it a practice to first find and memorize the location of the fire alarm and fire extinguishers on your floor. Examine them for operating instructions. Now, from your room walk the hallway again — this time to the nearest emergency exit, counting the number of doors to the *right* and then to the *left* of your room door to the nearest fire exit. Open the fire exit doors to check the route.

Remember in the event of fire or smoke, *never* use the elevator. Elevators may malfunction in a fire, may stop at fire floor or become a perfect well for smoke. When escaping, *always* use the stairs, but keep in mind it may sometimes be necessary or safer to remain in your room.

Inside your room, note if the windows are sealed or if they can be opened. Know how to shut off the air-conditioning system. Check the bathroom exhaust to make sure it works properly. The exhaust fan helps vent smoke. Put your room key and flashlight on the night-stand and always replace them there. In an emergency, they can be easily found to take with you.

Awakened Unexpectedly

If you're awakened from sleep by an unknown distur-bance, don't fall back asleep until you have fully satisfied yourself as to the cause. Make sure it's only a noisy party rather than the early stages of emergency.

If a hotel fire alarm or the smoke detector goes off or you smell smoke in your room, get your key and flashlight, roll off the bed to your hands and knees and crawl to the door. Gases and heat rise and you have a better chance for fresher air near the floor, generally about knee high. Feel the hallway door and handle. If they are not warm to touch, open the door slowly. Be prepared to slam it shut if the hallway is filled with smoke. If the hall is barely smoky, call the front desk or set off the nearest fire alarm, then crawl towards the nearest exit with flashlight and keys, closing the door behind you. A closed door provides a slow burning fire screen and slows the spread of fire. Stay close to the wall and floor as you move to the stairway exit, counting the doors as you go. If you encounter heavy smoke or an impassable situation, retrace your path to your room. You'll have your room key with you to get in.

Before entering the fire exit staircase, evaluate how smoky it is first. When you exit down the fire stairs, close the door behind you to prevent smoke from entering the stairwell. Hold onto the handrail firmly so you won't be knocked down in a rush of people. If you encounter smoke as you descend, turn around and walk up to the roof.

If the roof exit door is locked, evaluate whether you should stay put or retrace your steps. Otherwise, exit through the rooftop door, closing the door behind you. Find the windward side of the building and wait calmly until help arrives.

On the other hand, if your room's door or knob is too hot to the touch, do *not* open the door. The smoke or fire is too dangerously close to escape down the hallway. First, call the front desk, fire or police to notify them of your location. Turn off the air conditioning; turn on the bathroom exhaust fan and keep it running. Fill the bathtub and sink with cold water and start soaking towels. Use them to block the air vents and around the room door to prevent smoke from seeping into the room or use the duct tape to seal the room door. If the window can be opened, hang a sheet, blanket or bedspread out as a distress signal, but do not break a sealed window. If there is smoke outside, you may need to close it. Keep dousing the door and walls with water to keep them cool. If possible, prop the mattress against the door and secure it with a dresser. Keep wetting the mattress. Tie a wet towel around your nose and mouth as an effective smoke filter. Also, swinging a wet towel around the room helps clear the smoke.

As a last resort in hotel or high rise fire when the smoke may become too heavy and may overcome you, sit in the tub covered with a blanket and let the water from the shower run. The blanket will act as a filter and the water cools the heat.

Above all, stay calm. Don't panic. Overwhelming fear and foolish actions are deadly. You will need a clear head to follow through on these safety plans.

6

CHAPTER

PROTECTING YOUR PROPERTY AND SAVINGS

Let's make it harder for burglars to steal.

Although the odds of retrieving stolen articles are slim, your chances of getting them back increase greatly if you take these measures:

Mark Personal Property With Identification Numbers
Marking your property will make it more difficult for the thief to unload his haul through "fences."

Special engraving pens are available for inscribing metallic items, such as televisions, typewriters, power tools and cameras. The engraving pens can either be borrowed from your police department, the library, insurance agents, savings and loan associations or banks. Inexpensive pens can also be purchased in hobby or hardware stores.

— Use an identification number, usually your state's abbreviation (CA, TX, FL, NY, etc.), followed by your driver's license number.
— If you do not have a driver's license, use your area code and phone number as the identifying numbers.
— Place the identifying number near the item's serial number or on the upper right hand corner on the back and, if space permits, add your initials.

For soft goods, such as furs and leather coats, use ultraviolet or indelible ink. Carefully undo the lining, mark the item with your identification number and reattach the lining in the same manner as the original stitching. If a marked item is taken, remember to indicate the mark in your report to the police.

By engraving your property, police can easily contact you should it be recovered.

Make A Personal Property Inventory List

After marking your valuables, fill out a personal property list that shows make, model number, serial number and description of each article. (For your convenience, a form is provided at the back of this book.) Store the list in a safe fireproof place such as a safe deposit box or metal box. If you should ever need it, it is a handy record to have for police reports and insurance claims. Remember to add new items as they are purchased or acquired to keep your list current.

Take Pictures

Insurance agents recommend taking close-up pictures, preferably in color, of your valuables, especially those that are one of a kind or have a high replacement cost. Pictures of silver pieces, cameras and other photographic equipment, art works, and jewelry provide indisputable proof of possession for insurance recovery claims.

These decals can be obtained from your local police department or make your own. Place them on the front and rear doors and windows to help ward off potential burglars. Such warnings make burglary of your house less profitable for the thief.

PROTECTING YOUR SAVINGS

Cash is one of the most difficult of things to prove ownership. Avoid keeping large amounts of cash around the house and/or carrying it on your person.

— Arrange to have any regularly received checks, such as Social Security, dividend or pension checks, sent directly to your savings and loan association to be automatically deposited to your savings account. It saves a trip to deposit them and the checks or the cash from them cannot be stolen.

— *Beware of Confidence Games* Played by skilled con artists especially aimed at older female citizens, the two oldest ones are still very much in use.

"The Pigeon Drop"

In one version of this scheme, two very sharp, articulate operators attempt to swindle their potential victim or "pigeon" (victim) out of her life savings. The first operator engages the "pigeon" in random conversation. While they are talking, the second operator appears nearby, excitedly pretending to find a huge sum of money. Naturally, the "pigeon" and the first operator are attracted. Fake documentation indicates the money comes from an illegal or disreputable source and everyone tries to decide what to do with the money.

Through a series of clever conversational manipulations, one operator decides to consult a reputable "attorney" that she knows. Later, the victim is told that the "attorney" advises that they all may keep the money. However, in order to protect themselves, everyone should deposit a matching amount of good faith money in the "attorney's" safe. The operators escort the pigeon to her bank to withdraw the thousands of dollars in *cash*. The operators have supposedly done the same. All the money is placed in a single envelope and they go to the "attorney's" office building. One operator waits outside with the victim while the other goes inside. When the operator returns, the victim is told the "attorney" wants to see her. When she goes inside the building, she discovers that the attorney and his office are non-existent. And, of course, when she returns outside, the operators have vanished along with her life savings.

If you are approached with such a scheme, note the details of the person's appearance or vehicle license numbers. Report the incident to the police immediately. If you find yourself coerced right into your savings association's office, tell or write a note to the teller about the situation. Tellers are trained to watch for such crooked deals. After notifying superiors by pre-arranged signal, the teller will know how to stall until police arrive.

"The Phony Bank Examiner"

Victims, usually older single women, are taken in by their natural desire to cooperate with law enforcement officers against crime.

In this scheme, a telephone caller identifies himself as a bank examiner and cleverly manipulates the conversation so that the victim reveals the location of her savings account. The "bank examiner" then asks for her help in catching one of the employees. She is told to withdraw several thousand dollars and give the money to the "bank examiner" in exchange for a receipt. Needless to say, both the bank examiner and her money disappear.

If you are called for such a scheme, notify the police, bunco division, immediately.

Never, under any circumstances, withdraw large amounts of cash from your savings account. A cashier's check or money order will do just as well for any legitimate business transaction.

Use Safe Deposit Boxes

A safe deposit box is a good idea for protecting small valuables and important papers from fire and theft. What should be in your safe deposit box? A general rule of thumb is to keep irreplaceable or hard to replace papers in the box. Wills, birth and death certificates, adoption, military service or citizenship papers, investment certificates (stocks and bonds) and other government or court recorded papers should be there. Proof of ownership papers for your house and automobile, contracts, leases, patents and copyrights belong there too.

Be sure to include a copy of the Personal Property Inventory List in the safe deposit box along with the pictures and expensive jewelry, stamps and coins.

Avoid cluttering your box with insurance policies, cancelled checks, old income tax records, education and employment records, old passbooks and sentimental items. Keep them safely stored at home.

PROTECTING YOUR MOTOR VEHICLE
AND ITS CONTENTS

Not only does auto theft, either the car or its accessories, prove costly to you personally or by a general increase of insurance rates for all, but stolen vehicles can also be used in the commission of other crimes or injury to others. Remember to:

— Always leave your car's windows closed and doors locked even in your own driveway.

— Always take your keys with you on unattended street parking. Even in attended parking lots, leave only your ignition key. Otherwise, thieves can have duplicates made of your keys on the key ring to get inside your home or office later. Authorities recommend detachable key rings. With this type of key ring, you leave only your ignition key with the attendant; the rest are in your pocket or purse.

— Park and lock your car only in well lighted, heavily travelled streets. Even if auto thieves don't steal the car, there are those that can strip a car in minutes of its auto parts — hubcaps, radios, stereos, even bucket seats — for resale. Use the engraving pen to put your identification number on these highly desirable parts.

— If you own a camper or van, determine the location of the manufacturer's serial numbers and store the recorded numbers in your safe deposit box. Use the engraving pen to mark your identification number in inconspicuous places. Of course, make sure doors and windows in your camper or van have the same high quality locking devices as those you've installed in your home.

— Keep luggage, packages and valuables locked in the trunk and put them there *before* you reach your destination.
— Car thieves know all the obvious hiding spots for spare keys. Don't leave them in glove compartments, under the carpeting or in sun visors. The best bet is not to keep extra keys in your car.
— Anti-theft devices for all kinds of motor vehicles range from inexpensive to elaborate ones, available from auto supply stores. Among the many choices, there are door lock buttons, ignition kill switches and hood, trunk and hubcap alarms. If you own a sports car or an expensive small model, there's even an alarm to thwart auto thieves who pick up such cars with phony tow trucks! In the unhappy event your car or its parts are stolen, be sure to report it to the police at once so the information can be put on police computer networks.
— Buy and sell with caution. Except when buying from authorized dealers, have the police department verify the vehicle identification number and license number of any car you propose to buy. This check insures that the seller of the car really owns it.

When you sell your car, go with the prospective buyers for any road test. Make sure the purchase check has been safely verified and cleared before giving up the certificate of ownership.

PROTECTING MOTORCYCLES AND BICYCLES

Bikes of all kinds are favorite targets for theft. Always leave a motorcycle, moped or bike securely locked with heavy chains and strong padlocks. Using anything less invites theft for they are easily cut or pried.

- Chains must be of at least 5/16 inch hardened steel alloy; 3/8 inches for motorcycles. Links of continuous weld construction are important. The thicker the chain, the better.
- Padlocks also have to be sturdy enough to withstand a crowbar attack. (See Chapter 4 for minimum standards for padlocks.)
- Lock a bike in a public place by threading a chain through the frame and a wheel and then to a secure rack or pole. Keep the chain as high above the ground as possible.
- Store bikes in the garage attached to a 3/8 inch x 6 inch eye screw fastened to a stud. Place the eye screw at least three feet above the floor, making a pry bar much more difficult to use.

Investing in and using heavy duty chains and padlocks is less expensive than replacing the whole bike.

CHAPTER 7
PROTECTING YOURSELF

The key elements in preventing crimes against your person are *alertness* and *planning.* Both go a long way to minimize your risk of attack.

- Be alert as to who is standing near you, walking towards you or behind you, especially at night or in crowds.
- Don't look vulnerable, frightened or confused even if you are lost.
- Know where you are going and plan your route along well lighted, heavily travelled streets.
- Travel with a companion at night. If you must go alone, walk purposefully to your destination as if someone is waiting for you, checking for suspicious looking persons as you go.
- Carry a police whistle, shriek alarm or some other noisemaker with you and keep it handy.

- If you drive alone at night, always keep windows closed and doors locked. Never stop to pick up hitchhikers, no matter how innocent they look. Don't stop to give directions or assistance if you are flagged down. You can always drive to the nearest phone and call for assistance for them. If someone attempts to enter your car, spin quickly away and blow your horn.
- If you use the bus at night, get off at well lighted bus stops and arrange for someone to meet you.
- Call police if you observe strangers loitering about your residence, trying each door in your apartment building, slowly cruising cars or sitting in parked cars. Note personal description and make, color and license number of the car, time and location. Let the police evaluate your suspicions.
- Report any incident promptly to the police. They will want to know the attacker's approximate height, weight, age, color of eyes and hair, complexion, type and color of clothing, unusual voice characteristics (accent, language) and type of weapon, if any.

Continual alertness and preparation are your best defenses. The following suggestions are more good ideas to avoid potentially dangerous situations.

Preventing Muggings, Pickpocketing and Purse-Snatching.

Before You Leave Home
- Don't carry large sums of cash with you. Take only what you will need for the day.
- Distribute keys, credit cards and money on your person, perhaps hidden in various pockets and yes, even inside an article of clothing. If you are robbed, it will lessen your losses and you'll still have your house and auto keys.

— Don't wear expensive jewelry or wristwatches just for a shopping trip. Keep chains tucked underneath clothing. Turn rings around your fingers so the stones don't show.
— Don't carry a purse whenever it is possible. If you must carry one, select a short handled purse and hold it close to you, tucked in the bend of your elbow. If you're suspicious that someone is following you, hold it upside down, hand on the clasp. That way, if it is snatched, the contents will spill out and circumvent the theft.

When wearing shoulder bags, place the strap diagonally across your shoulder. Put your coat on over your purse.

Never leave your purse unattended, even for a second. Keep it on your lap in the movies or in a restaurant. When shopping, never put your purse on the store's counter or in the market's shopping cart as you select merchandise.
— Men: Insert a short comb in your wallet, teeth side up, before putting it in your back pocket. The comb teeth will catch on the pocket lining if someone tries to remove it. Or carry your wallet inside your jacket or in a front pocket.

On the Street

— Avoid dark and deserted streets, shaded areas, or short cuts through alleys, open spaces or behind buildings.
— Especially at night, walk near the curb, away from buildings and watch for slowly moving cars.
— Carry a dependable flashlight, police whistle or other noisemaker. Lights and noise scare away potential trouble.
— If you think you are being followed, go into the nearest open place of business and phone police. If an open business is not available, make as much noise as possible by shouting and screaming for help. You may feel silly, but in an actual situation, it will scare off any would-be attacker.

When Returning Home
— Take a few seconds to observe any suspicious-looking persons about before entering your house or apartment building. If you do, don't go inside. Go somewhere else and call police.
— Once inside your apartment building, watch for strangers loitering around. Don't enter your apartment; they might follow you and shove you inside. Instead, ring a neighbor's bell and act like a visitor until he is gone. Notify the police if he does not leave.

At Home
— Never open the door for strangers no matter what the excuse. Do not depend on the chain guard for protection; determined burglars have been known to rip them off.
— Use the peephole and speak through the door.
— Do not open the door for deliverymen with unexpected packages; uncalled servicemen or strangers seeking directions, claiming accidents or needing the telephone. Through the closed door, offer to make that call. If they are not agreeable, inform them that you are calling the police to assist them.

In A Confrontation
Experts agree it's generally best not to resist. Many women have been seriously injured while fighting off purse-snatchers. By keeping your valuables out of your purse, you have not given the thief anything that cannot be replaced. If you are able to, make a careful observation of the purse-snatcher to describe to police later.

If a mugger confronts you with a weapon or threat of physical violence, most of us are not trained or have the prowess to overpower him. Your cash and property are not as important as your life. Reacting intelligently in such a situation will preserve life and limb. The rest is replaceable.

Preventing Rape

Women living or travelling alone need to take these extra precautions:

— When arriving home by taxi or private auto, ask the driver to wait until you are safely inside.

— Have your house key ready so your door can be opened immediately.

— When walking alone, keep alert for approaching cars. Never accept rides from strangers. If you are threatened, scream and run in the opposite direction from the car. He'd have to turn around to pursue you.

— Always make sure your car is well maintained before setting out on a trip. Periodic checks of tires, battery, water, oil, fan belts and hoses will lessen the risk of being caught alone in unfamiliar or isolated areas. Travel with more than enough gas to get where you're going and a safe return home. If you travel a great deal by auto, it even pays to learn how to fix a flat tire and try it once before you need to.

— When driving alone, and you think you're being followed, do not drive into your driveway. Head for a hotel, restaurant, a parking lot with attended parking or a crowded, busy area. Do not be forced off or pulled over to the side of the road in your car. If possible, write down the car make, license number and description of the driver and report the incident to the police.

— If your car becomes disabled in an isolated area or on the freeway, raise the hood, turn on your hazard lights, tie a white cloth to the aerial and sit inside with the windows rolled up and doors locked until help arrives. Leave the windows up while you talk to whomever approaches. Ask them to send aid rather than going with strangers to obtain it. Major roads are patrolled 24 hours a day.

— Whenever you return to your car, check the back seat and floor before getting in to make sure no one has broken in and is hiding, waiting for you.

— Make sure your home or apartment garage and entrances are well lighted.

— List only your last name and initial in phone directories and on mailboxes or "invent" a roommate or husband to create the impression you are not alone.
— Avoid mentioning that you live alone, especially to unknown callers and strangers at the door.
— Keep lights on in two or more rooms to indicate the presence of other persons.
— Don't enter an apartment house elevator with strange men. Wait in the lobby for the next one. If there's a basement in the building, send the elevator down there first and wait for its return empty before entering it. If a suspicious looking stranger gets on the elevator you are on, get off at the next floor.
— Never remain alone in the apartment's laundry room. Enter the room cautiously and leave quickly.
— If you are attacked, there are no restrictions. Scream, yell, kick and fight — anything to ward him off. Umbrellas, keys, ball point pens, high-heeled shoes or any pointed object make effective weapons. Cries for help, whistles, lamp breaking — make the noise loud enough to attract attention and, in most cases, discourage the criminal.

However, if there's a weapon involved, you then have to make a personal decision whether or not to resist the attacker, depending on your strength, the situation and the psychological state of the attacker. An intelligent judgment is your best defense.

Preventing Theft When You Travel
When you travel, the same precautions apply even more so in unfamiliar cities and countries.
— Obtain traveler's checks before you leave. Keep a record of the traveler's checks numbers safely stored in a separate place from the checks themselves and cross off the numbers as you use them. If they are stolen or lost, you'll have your check numbers easily available for prompt replacement.

— Luggage tags should have only your last name visible or use a business card instead. Thieves have been known to read luggage tags in airports and hotels to identify unoccupied homes. Staple the ends of the tags so the paper cannot be removed easily. Also, put a business card inside each piece of luggage.
— Keep a close watch on all your luggage as it sits waiting on airport or hotel sidewalks. Keep your valuables with you at all times in a small suitcase.
— Use a travel lock to safeguard bulky valuables like cameras and furs in a hotel. It attaches to bureau drawers and closet doors when you're out for the day. At night, when you're sleeping, it can secure the room's door from the inside.
— Stay on well lighted main streets and public areas.
— Do not hire unauthorized guides off the streets.
— Use hotel safes for deposit of expensive jewelry, wristwatches, keys or large amounts of cash for safekeeping, whenever the items are not used and even if you plan on being in your room or in the hotel. The clerk will give you a deposit slip and key to the safe deposit box and your key is required to open it along with your authorized signature. Most hotels provide this service free of charge.

In the Unlikely Event You Are Taken Hostage

The chances that you or a member of your family will be kidnapped or fall into a hostage situation are very slight.
— Do not give out information about yourself or your family habits freely to "survey takers" or callers. Caution family members to do the same.
— Be aware of strange or suspicious persons or cars near your home.
— Do not open the door to an unexpected delivery or repairman until you are positive of his business.
— Don't be fooled by a "telephone company official" who calls to ask, on the pretext of fixing lines, that you not answer the phone for the next few hours. The phone company does not make such requests.
— Carefully check any "emergency" phone calls from strangers that would get your family members into unescorted or unfamiliar situations.

— Advise your children's school officials not to release them during school hours without your personal appearance or consent.

Some hostage situations such as skyjacking and store hold-ups are beyond preventative planning.

If the improbable occurs and you're taken hostage, experts advise several things to protect your personal safety and increase the likelihood you will emerge unharmed:

— Remain calm. In the beginning, hostage-takers are on edge, insecure and aggressive. Do nothing to antagonize them. Obey reasonable instructions politely. This is not the time to play tough or try to fool them.

— Be observant without appearing obvious. Note the approximate time, locations and physical description of the hostage-takers. Besides the standard descriptions of hair, eye color, height, weight, age, build and clothing, watch for unusual jewelry, scars, tattoos and type of voices.

  Even if you are blindfolded, listen for characteristic noises of your surroundings: bells, airplanes, motors, typewriters, unusual odors — anything to help investigating officers later. If you are moved from place to place, concentrate on details of routes, directions, time and methods of transportation for reporting later.

— Leave fingerprints at the scene on smooth surfaces of metal or plastic. Some hostage victims have unobtrusively left buttons, cuff links, threads from their clothing or personal objects from their pockets. If possible, secretly take items from the scene with you. Police will then have critical evidence for successful prosecution later.

— If a confrontation between the hostage takers and law enforcement officers seems near, prepare to stay out of the way as much as possible.

In these situations, alert, observant, and calm hostages have saved lives and led to the capture and conviction of the criminals.

EMERGENCY ITEMS CHECKLIST

Always keep these items on hand at home:

1. Portable radio with extra batteries.
2. Flashlight with extra batteries and bulbs.
3. First Aid Kit — including specific medicines and extra glasses needed for members of your household.
4. First Aid Book.
5. Fire Extinguisher.
6. Adjustable wrench for turning off gas and water.
7. Smoke detector properly installed.
8. Portable fire escape ladder for homes/apartments with multiple floors.
9. Bottled water — sufficient for the number of members in your household.
10. Canned and dried foods sufficient for a week for each member of your household. Note: Both water and food should be rotated into normal meals of household so as to keep freshness. Canned goods have a normal shelf-life of one year for maximum freshness.
11. Non-electric can opener.
12. Portable stove such as butane or charcoal. Note: Use of such stoves should not take place until it is determined that there is no gas leak in the area. Charcoal should be burned only out of doors. Use of charcoal indoors will lead to carbon monoxide poisoning.
13. Matches.
14. Telephone numbers of police, fire and doctor.

Plus knowing the location of gas, water and electricity mains and how to turn them off.

Source: AMERICAN RED CROSS

CHAPTER 8

PROTECTION IN NATURAL DISASTERS

Each region of the country has its share of natural disasters. The potential damage from earthquakes, hurricanes, tornadoes, flash flooding and snow storms can be minimized if we are prepared beforehand and know how to respond during them. Physical and mental emergency preparedness saves lives, lessens property damage and reduces panic and fear.

EARTHQUAKES

When an earthquake strikes, the solid earth may pitch and roll like a ship or may shudder in a series of sharp jolts.

The motion is frightening but unless something falls on you, earthquakes are not dangerous in themselves. It is their effect (flying glass, overturned furnishings, fallen power lines, broken gas lines, unsafe human action) that causes the casualties.

Also, be prepared for "aftershocks," a series of smaller jolts or shudders that may occur hours and/or days after the primary earthquake.

The American Red Cross and government authorities recommend:

Before An Earthquake Strikes

Prepare your home to reduce injury and property damage:

— Secure water heaters and other gas appliances. These can be strapped to a wall or bolted down so that gas lines and appliance connections will not be broken during the shaking. Use flexible connections wherever possible.

— Put large or heavy objects on low shelves. Much damage is the result of such objects falling from high places. Install locks on cabinet doors, especially if its contents are valuable or sentimental breakables.

— Secure bookcases and cabinets to walls.

— Relocate beds so they are not under chimneys or in basements. During a quake, basements are especially prone to flooding by water from a water heater or pool.

— A home foundation should be continuous reinforced concrete and the wood frame bolted to the concrete will reduce structural damages considerably.

— Stock minimum emergency equipment: flashlight, battery-power transister radio, first aid kit and a fire extinguisher. (See chart on page 88.)

Prepare your family:

— Immunization of family members should be kept up-to-date.

— Teach family members where the shut-off valves of gas, water and electric lines are *and* how to turn them off. Family members should also know how to respond during and after earthquakes. Occasional home earthquake drills would be good reminders and lessen panic if an earthquake does strike.

— Decide on a common meeting place after an earthquake.

During An Earthquake

— Keep calm and avoid rash actions.

— If indoors, stay inside. Do not try to walk. Get low to the ground and stay where you are during the shaking. Take cover under a table, desk or bed and near inside walls, corners or under doorways. Stay away from windows, mirrors, chimneys, high bookcases, bookshelves or anything that might topple over. In a high-rise office building or store, take shelter under a desk or sturdy object. It's best not to run to crowded exits which may already be jammed with frightened people.

— If outdoors, do not run. Move calmly away from buildings, walls, power poles and other potential falling objects. Head towards the nearest open area and stay there until the shaking stops.
— In a vehicle, drive away from underpasses, overpasses and bridges. Stop in a safe area and stay in the vehicle.

After The Shaking Stops
— Check for injuries. Render first aid.
— Check your house's power and utility lines carefully. If damaged, shut off at main valve. If you detect a gas leak, shut off the main gas valve. Open the windows and do not use light switches or any matches, lighters or electrical appliances. Sparks can ignite gas from broken lines. If light is needed, use a flashlight. Then leave the residence and report the damage to authorities. Stay outside until the utility official says it is safe to reenter.
— If electrical wiring is shorting out, switch off the electric supply at the main switch.
— If water supply mains are damaged, shut off the main valve. Emergency water can be obtained from melting ice cubes, toilet tanks, water heaters and canned vegetables. Check sewage lines before permitting flushing of toilets.
— Turn on your radio or television for emergency bulletins and instructions. Use your battery radio if necessary.
— Clean up spilled medicines and other potentially dangerous substances.
— Check closets and cupboards carefully by opening doors slowly, watching for falling objects.
— Check your chimney and foundation for cracks and damage to spot potential safety problems during aftershocks.
— If power is off, check your freezer and refrigerator and plan to use up foods which spoil quickly. Outdoor charcoal broilers can be used for emergency cooking out of doors only!
— Don't use the telephone except for emergencies.
— Outside, do not touch downed power lines or objects touching them.
— Don't sightsee, especially on waterfront areas where seismic sea waves can still occur. Keep the street clear for emergency vehicles. If you live in a low lying coastal area, head for the high ground until the officials say it is safe to return.

- Aftershocks can cause additional damage. Be prepared mentally and in your living arrangements for them.
- Cooperate fully with civil authorities and public safety officials. Stay out of disaster areas unless your help has been specifically requested.

WIND/WATER STORMS

Each year thousands of wind and water storms rip through the land, racking up billions of dollars in property damage. The cost of life, of course, is incalculable.

Too often, newcomers to the area are simply unaware of how terrible these storms can be. Inexperienced in their ways, the newly settled resident, either through disbelief or ignorance, does not heed the warnings nor prepare adequately. By the same token, long established area residents have hazy memories; the last killer storm may have been a dozen or more years ago. Different conditions now exist; new research has uncovered better emergency preparation techniques for today. For both natives and newcomers, the most dangerous thing about natural disaster is a false sense of security.

HURRICANES

By definition, a hurricane is a large, violent, circular storm with heavy winds and rains. Hurricane winds are 74 miles per hour or more with gusts up to 200 miles per hour. The hurricane's area can span several hundred miles and its path is unpredictable.

The most lethal part of a hurricane is when the *storm surge,* a great dome of water often 50 miles wide, hits the coastline, sweeping away everything in its path. Nine out of ten hurricane fatalities are caused by the storm surge. The stronger the hurricane, the higher the storm surge will be.

(Tornadoes and flooding often accompany hurricanes. Read the following sections for additional safety measures to take.)

Hurricane season in the southeastern United States runs June through December with the heart of the season occurring August through October. Although the Gulf Coast is particularly vulnerable, hurricanes are also a threat along the Atlantic seaboard.

Modern detection and tracking devices help warn residents of potentially dangerous storms. The National Weather Service in cooperation with the National Hurricane Center in Miami keeps close watch during hurricane season and issues advisory bulletins when hurricanes approach land.

A *hurricane watch* is issued when a hurricane threatens coastal areas. With a lead time of 24 to 36 hours, a watch signals that residents should make plans for evacuation.

A *hurricane warning* is dispatched when the hurricane winds reach 74 m.p.h. and/or dangerously high waves are expected in a specific coastal area with 24 hours. Preparation plans should be put into action immediately.

If you live in a coastal area serviced by few roads, early evacuation is imperative. If a hurricane does strike your community, the roads may become too clogged with traffic for a safe retreat.

Before Hurricane Season
Preparations should begin before June.
— Check and restock your three day supply of nonperishable food and your first aid kit. Have a battery powered radio and flashlights on hand as well as a supply of fresh, extra batteries.
— Protect from flying glass by taping windows and glass doors with heavy duty tape.
— Install storm shutters.
— Trim back dead wood from trees.

— Know the safest route inland and the location of official shelters.
— Know your community's emergency signals: sirens, bells, radio channels — and what safety plans will be in effect.
— Boatowners should know where their boats should be moved.
— Know the storm surge history and elevation of your area.

The Hurricane Watch
When a hurricane watch is issued:
— Stay tuned to your radio for the latest bulletins.
— Fuel your car in case evacuation becomes necessary.
— Check supplies of special medicines or drugs.
— Take in or tie down loose outdoor objects such as porch and lawn furniture, garbage cans, garden tools, signs, toys, flower pots. In a full gale, these may become as deadly as bullet shots. Tape, board or shutter windows. Wedge sliding doors so they won't be lifted from their tracks.
— Store drinking water in clean bathtubs and other containers. The water supply may become interrupted or contaminated by the storm.
— Moor your boat or move it to safe shelter.

The Hurricane Warning
Generally, if you live on a coastline or offshore area, in a mobile home, near a river or flood plain, you should prepare to leave.
— Shut off water and gas at their main valves and electrical power at the main switch.
— Take pets inside and leave food and water for them.
— Continue listening to the radio or television for the latest bulletins. If authorities recommend evacuation, leave the area immediately! Take small valuables and important documents but travel light. Lock up the house, leave as early in the daylight hours as possible and drive carefully to the nearest shelter using recommended evacuation routes.

If you live inland on high ground in a sturdy dwelling, you can consider staying home unless instructed otherwise. At home, continue to stay tuned to official reports. Board up garage and porch doors. Move valuables to upper floors in case of flooding. Turn up refrigerator to maximum cold and keep its door closed as much as possible.

Fill containers with several day's supply of drinking water. Take pets inside and stay indoors — downwind and away from the windows. Beware of the eye of the hurricane in which winds will suddenly decrease and skies may clear. When the eye passes, the winds will blow from the opposite directions as strong or stronger than before.

After The Hurricane Passes

Once the all-clear signal is given that it is safe to leave the public shelter, drive home carefully. Keep tuned to local radio stations for routes to use and disaster areas to avoid. Coastal roads may be washed out from beneath the pavement or can collapse under the weight of a car. Keep away from dangling wires and flooded low spots.

At home, check for damaged water, sewer and electrical lines or gas leaks and report them. If the electricity is off, check for food spoilage. Be cautious of tap water; it may have been contaminated. Survey the building for damage and make any emergency repairs.

TORNADOES

Each year, the United States experiences over 600 tornadoes. Their fierce whirling winds cause an estimated 250 million dollars in property damage annually. Although tornadoes have occurred in all 50 states, the most frequent and violent ones sweep across the American Midwest, most often in Texas, Oklahoma, Kansas, Nebraska and Missouri.

The height of tornado season is in spring, (April, May, June) usually in the late afternoon of a hot day. Often accompanied by heavy rains and dangerous lightning, tornadoes are highly erratic and difficult to predict. However, the National Severe Storms Forecast Center operated by the National Weather Service in Kansas City, Missouri, does notify citizens when and where they are most likely to occur.

Tornadoes cause damage to buildings by the explosive effect of their high winds. Flying debris picked up by its characteristic swirling causes further destruction.

A *tornado watch* bulletin is issued for areas about 140 miles wide and 200 miles long when meterological conditions indicate a tornado is possible. Residents in or near a watch area should be on the lookout for threatening conditions and report a tornado sighting to police. Mobile homeowners should seek sturdier shelter before threatening conditions approach.

A *tornado warning* indicates a tornado has actually been sighted. Stay tuned to the radio or television for further bulletins — and keep an eye on the sky. The danger signals are: severe thunderstorms with frequent lightning, heavy rains, strong winds, power failure, hail, a deafening roaring noise and the familiar funnel shaped cloud. The warning also reports the "downstream" — the path the tornado might take. However, warnings may not always be given, especially for the small sized mini-tornadoes, so residents should be very aware of their possibility in a strong thunderstorm. When a warning is issued in your area, take cover immediately. It may be a matter of minutes before the twister strikes.

Long before the tornado approaches your home, open the windows a little and prepare to take cover. In a home with a basement, the safest places are under stairwells or furniture below ground, away from windows and chimneys. For those buildings without basements, seek the lowest level in a central portion of the structure. Choose an interior closet first or, if necessary, an interior hallway. A small interior bathroom is another good choice because the plumbing lines act as a safety cage. Small rooms are better than larger ones; there is less danger of the ceiling collapsing. There is less likelihood of flying glass, debris or ceiling damage in this section.

- Wherever you are, cover your head with your arms and your body with a blanket to protect against flying glass.
- Mobile homes, even when properly tied down, afford little protection. Leave immediately, and if there's no time to seek shelter, lie in a nearby ditch, away from the mobile home and electric lines.
- If you're driving, it may not be possible to outrun the tornado because its path is unpredictable. Tornado winds are strong enough to pick up automobiles. Stop the car and get into the nearest shelter. If there's not enough time or you're driving or walking in open country, head for the nearest ditch, ravine or shallow depression and lie face down with your arms over your head.

Special Alert. Mobile Home Dwellers

Winds are a serious threat to mobile homes; damage can range from small dents to total destruction. Tornadoes and hurricanes blow mobile homes off their blocks, but even strong sudden gusts can tip one over.

By their long, low and light design, mobile homes are particularly vulnerable in wind storms. Also, appliances grouped along one wall shift the home's center of gravity toward one side and make them more likely to shift or roll.

Before buying a mobile home, look for built-in safety features such as factory installed anchor straps.

In a mobile home park, choose a level lot with a solid concrete foundation and steel anchor locations.
- Plant trees, bushes and small hills to shield your home.
- Place your home so that narrow end faces prevailing winds, reducing the surface area exposed to the impact of the wind.
- If you put a skirt around the bottom of your mobile home, make it an openwork or lattice one. Winds blow through these instead of meeting resistance.
- Check that the mobile home park has a below ground shelter located underneath the park's community hall or permanent residence.
- Install "tiedowns." Tiedowns anchor a mobile home to the ground with sturdy wire, with proper blocking and spacing underneath and at each end of the mobile home. Check with your mobile home manufacturer or local civil defense preparedness unit for specific recommendations. Professional installation will take

into account the length of the mobile home, the surrounding soil conditions and the area's maximum expected wind speeds. Don't overlook patio awnings, cabanas and expando units in your tiedown plan.

— Get your neighbors to properly tie down their homes too. Then yours will be less likely to be damaged by an unanchored one blowing into it.

In *severe weather,* keep informed of winds and flood conditions and prepare to leave immediately. If there's time, pack breakables, including medicines, in well padded cartons and store them on the floor. Remove bulbs from lamps and tape mirrors and windows. Lamps and mirrors can be stored in the bathtub with a blanket underneath. Disconnect electrical, sewer and water lines. Drain water faucets and leave them open. Turn off gas bottles at the tank. Anchor or stow away outside furniture and garbage cans.

. . .and most importantly, allow enough time to seek shelter elsewhere.

FLOODING

Even as it moves inland, the hurricane's torrential rains can dump 6 to 20 inches and more of water in the area it crosses, causing massive flooding. But flood waters also rise from melting snow, ice break-up, earthquakes and dam ruptures. Whether seasonal or sudden, the water's raging torrents rapidly overflow river beds and drainage channels, uprooting trees, smashing structures, overturning cars and dislodging boulders as it rolls along its deadly course. The debris it carries along causes even more damage.

When flooding is very sudden, when water moves very fast or the water level rises quickly, it is called a *FLASH FLOOD*. Never underestimate the power and rapidity of a flash flood. Take quick action; you may have only seconds to escape.

The National Weather Service monitors river beds and storms for these killer floods and issues two kinds of citizen alerts:

FLASH FLOOD WATCH means a threat of flooding exists.

FLASH FLOOD WARNING signals that such a flood is likely or is occurring.

Before the Flood
— Find out from local authorities, perhaps the City or the County Engineer, the elevation of your property or building in relation to nearby waterways.
— Become familiar with the area's flood history.
— Know your area's designated shelters.
— Stock emergency supplies.
— Keep sandbags, plywoods, plastic sheeting and lumber on hand.
— Have check valves installed in the sewer lines from your home to prevent flood water from backing up into drains.
— Stay extra alert for weather reports; watch thunder and lightning as signs of distant heavy rainfall.

The Flood Warning
— If there's time, move essential valuables to high ground.
— Store drinking water in sealed containers.
— Move quickly and early to a safe area before you're cut off by flood water, but do not attempt to cross a flowing stream on foot where water is above your knees.
— If you're driving, beware of water of unknown depth in dips in the road. Not only could your car be submerged but the road could already be washed out. Never drive over bridges covered with water; you could be swept away. If your car stalls or is trapped in water, leave it and get to high grounds if you can do so safely. Stay off hill tops and away from all trees, lightning could strike. Don't drive at night; you won't be able to see rising water.

— Campers should be especially aware of rain, thunder and lightning in nearby hills. If you're camping in a remote area, never sleep on low ground. Tune in for latest weather reports and prepare to move out fast. Know where the high ground is, away from natural riverbeds and drainage canals, and how to get there.

After The Flood
— Test drinking water for purity and do not use fresh food that has come in contact with flood water.
— Stay away from the disaster area. Emergency crews need to do their work unhampered by sightseers.
— Beware of electrical wires and equipment in wet area. Report broken utility lines to authorities.
— Stay tuned for further news of additional flooding.

MUD SLIDES
In some areas of the country, the earth gives way after the rains, floods and brush fires, sometimes long afterwards. Deepseated failures well beyond the rainy and fire seasons can cause massive amounts of soil to slide, covering or toppling houses in its path. Hillside residents should plan ahead.
— Find out your property's soil characteristics with the help of a county or nearby university's geological engineer. It may be necessary to mix the soil with cement or lime to increase the surface cohesiveness and strength.
— Install an effective drainage system to divert heavy rain water before it soaks into the ground.
— Plant nearby slopes with appropriate vegetation to hold the soil and reduce the amount of water penetrating into the ground.
— Local authorities will have more suggestions based on their familiarity with your area's soil conditions.

WINTER WARNINGS

Each winter season, many unnecessary deaths occur because of foolhardy or hazardous actions. Know winter's danger and how to prepare yourself accordingly.

Winter Storms

Keep aware of weather conditions. A forecast of a severe storm in the next several hours or the following day should help you avoid getting caught in it or at least to properly cope with it. The National Weather Service uses these terms:

— *Ice storm, sleet, freezing rain, freezing drizzle* means a coating of ice is expected. Road and streets are slippery and driving and walking should be avoided.

— *Heavy snow* means four to six inches or more is expected in the next 12 hours or six or more inches in the next 24 hours. Along with *snow flurries, snow squalls,* and *blowing and drifting snow,* these warnings signal reduced visibility and slippery or blocked roads.

— *Blizzard* is the most dangerous of all winter storms. Winds of at least 35 miles per hour, temperatures of 20°F or below, considerable falling or blowing snow over an extended period of time frequently reduce visibility to less than a quarter of a mile. If possible, it's best to stay home.
— *Severe blizzard* means wind roar at 45 miles per hour, the temperature drops below 10°F and dense snow falls. Stay inside and stay tuned for further weather advisories.

Remember, a *watch* means a winter storm is approaching; a *warning* means it is imminent.

Winter Preparations
At home
— Install heat saving energy conservation devices: water heater blankets, weather stripping and attic insulation. Your local utility company offers free advice on how to cut down on fuel bills.
— During winter, keep an adequate supply of heating fuel on hand and use it sparingly. Regular supplies of electricity and gas may be cut off in a storm.
— Have some sort of emergency heating equipment on hand, such as a kerosene space heater or camp stove, and an adequate supply of coal or wood for a fireplace.
— Close off infrequently used rooms until the emergency is over.
— Stock emergency supplies.
— Dress properly for the cold weather. Several layers of loose fitting, warm clothing are better than one thin layer. Mittens are warmer than gloves. Fifty percent of the body's heat is lost through the head, so wear a warm hat or cap, even indoors if necessary. Outdoors, wear a hood muffler to cover your head and face to protect your lungs from extremely cold air.
— Avoid over-exertion. Cold weather alone places extra demands on your heart. Unaccustomed physical exercise such as shoveling snow, pushing a car or walking far increases the risk of heart attack or stroke. Avoid these activities, but, if you must work, work slowly. Stop *before* you get tired. Heart attacks are a major cause of death during and after winter storms.

Driving

— Keep travel to a minimum. Use public transportation rather than your automobile.

— If a car trip, even a short one, is imperative, make sure your auto is in good condition, properly serviced, fueled and equipped with snow tires or chains. Always try to take another person with you and that someone else knows your schedule, route and estimated time of arrival at your destination. Travel by daylight on major highways. Keep the car radio on to listen to current road and weather conditions. Drive slowly and cautiously. If the storm ahead looks bad, stop and seek shelter or turn back. A blizzard is no time to take deadly chances.

— In winter, you should have the following emergency equipment stored in your car's trunk and glove compartment:

☐ blankets
☐ emergency road flares
☐ candles, matches, flashlights and extra batteries
☐ portable radio
☐ high energy foods: raisins, peanuts, chocolates or hard candy
☐ a first aid kit (with several dimes taped to it for emergency pay phone use)
☐ booster cables
☐ tow chain or heavy duty rope
☐ sand
☐ long handled shovel
☐ windshield scraper
☐ extra sets of heavy mittens, woolen socks, winter headgear, overshoes, sweaters, change of clothing
☐ paper towels, tissues, bright colored cloth
☐ extra gasoline in an approved container
☐ knife (for slitting seat cushions)

Even with your best safety precautions, if you are stuck in an unexpected blizzard, the car breaks down or stalls or get lost, keep calm and *stay in your car.* Think through your actions and do them slowly and carefully. First, put out a trouble signal by tying a brightly colored cloth to your antenna and raising it high. Remember to:

— Keep a window open slightly for ventilation at all times.
— Run your engine and heater for warmth sparingly. The open window should be downwind to avoid carbon monoxide poisoning. Warm engines that are shut off cause snow melt to flood the ignition system. Either run the engine in shortly spaced intervals or keep it continuously running. An engine running all night without stopping burns up about eight gallons of gas.
— Do not eat snow; melt it first. Snow chills the body too quickly. Do not drink alcohol. Liquor accelerates heat loss.
— Wrap feet in wool blankets or stuffing from seat cushions cut open with your emergency knife.
— Turn on the dome light at night so work crews can spot you.
— Do blood circulating exercises in your car: clap hands, move legs and arms vigorously from time to time.
— Keep watch. Don't let all occupants of the car sleep at once.
— The worst thing to do in a blizzard is to get out of the car and walk around looking for aid. Stay put and stay calm; help is on its way.

HYPOTHERMIA

Hypothermia occurs when a cold environment overcomes the body's ability to keep warm.

Often overlooked and unreported as a cause of winter deaths, hypothermia has been called a silent killer. Exposure hypothermia claims many lives because the victims, especially senior citizens, didn't know they were freezing to death.

Older people, especially those over 65, are particularly susceptible because they don't respond as effectively to the stress of cold. About 10 per cent of people over 65 have a defect in their body temperature regulation system so that they do not shiver, a reliable warning signal of danger. However, people of all ages have fallen victim to hypothermia even though they never really felt cold.

— Know the danger signals of approaching hypothermia: thirst, dizziness, an overwhelming desire for sleep, numbness, fatigue and pale skin.
— Keep warm by wearing the right clothing for weather. Several layers of heat retaining wool clothing insulate the body better than one thick jacket.
— Put on an extra sweater (even if you don't feel cold) when room temperature drops below 60°-65°.
— Eat warm foods as a part of every meal. Drink plenty of fluids (1-1½ quarts of liquid a day). When people get cold, they tend to eat and drink less, intensifying the effect of the cold.
— Don't drink alcohol. Liquor accelerates heat loss.
— Move around. Light exercise such as walking or stretching increases the body's heat production.
— Outdoors, know the limits of your strength. Don't over-exert yourself and guard against wetness and sweating. Take along quick-energy snacks and an extra change of dry socks and clothes.

If you're lost or stranded, keep calm in order to make clearheaded decisions. Stay as warm and dry as possible. Concentrate on seeking shelter in the immediate vicinity for it's a waste of body heat and energy to wander all over. Seek a cave or overhanging ridge to protect against wind chill. Line the area with tree boughs and if possible, start a fire. Keep energy up by eating and drinking and moving around every so often. Always try to signal for help and get out of the cold as fast as possible.

CHAPTER 9
NOW THAT YOU KNOW

The numerous suggestions and cautions covered in this book may seem too much to remember or act upon — until you become a victim.

Rather than closing the proverbial barn door, take the time *now* to secure your house and property and prepare yourself and your family.

Realistically, there is no 100% guarantee against burglary, attack, fire or natural disaster. But, with a minimum of effort and forethought, you can reduce damage from any of these threats. Making it harder for the burglar to enter, the fire to start, or the natural disaster to destroy is something that is easily within our abilities ... and it begins with each one of us.

WARNING!
THESE PREMISES
ARE PROTECTED
All contents have permanent
registered code marks
They can be traced
By Law Enforcement Agencies
Operation
HomeGuard

APPENDIX

SOURCES FOR ADDITIONAL AID AND INFORMATION:

Crime Prevention Unit — Local Police Department

Fire Prevention Officer or Bureau — Local Fire Department

Emergency Preparedness — State office or local office of the American Red Cross

Victim of Crime Assistance and Compensation — the local police department can direct you to the appropriate state agency or write: National Organization for Victim Assistance (NOVA), 1757 Park Road, N.W., Washington D.C. 20010

National Weather Service
National Oceanic and Atmospheric Administration
U.S. Department of Commerce
Washington D.C. 20230

National Fire Protection Association
Batterymarch Park
Quincy, Massachusetts 02269

(Put this Personal Property inventory list in a safe place . . . it's a great shopping list for thieves.)

Date _____

Belonging to: _____

Driver's License # _____

AUTOMOBILE, MOTORCYCLE, SCOOTER

Marked with

Make	Color	Lic. No.	Serial No.	CDL #

BICYCLE

Make	Color	Lic. No.	Frame No.	CDL #

GUNS

Make	Caliber	Serial No.	CDL #

TELEVISION, RADIO, STEREO, TAPE RECORDER, ETC.

Item	Make	Serial No.	CDL #

TYPEWRITERS, OFFICE MACHINES, SMALL APPLIANCES

Item	Make	Serial No.	CDL #

CAMERA, BINOCULARS, SPORTING GOODS, SEWING MACHINE, WATCHES

Item	Make	Serial No.	CDL #

POWER TOOLS & SPECIAL EQUIPMENT

Item	Make	Serial No.	CDL #

(Put this Personal Property inventory list in a safe place . . .
it's a great shopping list for thieves.)

OTHER PROPERTY MARKED WITH YOUR
DRIVER'S LICENSE NO. _____

Item	Make

OTHER PROPERTY MARKED WITH YOUR
DRIVER'S LICENSE NO. _____

Item	Make